Practical and Effective Management of Libraries

CHANDOS
INFORMATION PROFESSIONAL SERIES

Series Editor: Ruth Rikowski
(e-mail: Rikowskigr@aol.com)

Chandos' new series of books are aimed at the busy information professional. They have been specially commissioned to provide the reader with an authoritative view of current thinking. They are designed to provide easy-to-read and (most importantly) practical coverage of topics that are of interest to librarians and other information professionals. If you would like a full listing of current and forthcoming titles, please visit our website at www.chandospublishing.com or e-mail info@chandospublishing.com or telephone +44 (0) 1223 891358.

New authors: we are always pleased to receive ideas for new titles; if you would like to write a book for Chandos, please contact Dr Glyn Jones on e-mail gjones@chandospublishing.com or telephone number +44 (0) 1993 848726.

Bulk orders: some organisations buy a number of copies of our books. If you are interested in doing this, we would be pleased to discuss a discount. Please e-mail info@chandospublishing.com or telephone +44 (0) 1223 891358.

Practical and Effective Management of Libraries: Integrating case studies, general management theory and self-understanding

RICHARD J. MONIZ JR

Chandos Publishing

Oxford · Cambridge · New Delhi

Chandos Publishing
TBAC Business Centre
Avenue 4
Station Lane
Witney
Oxford OX28 4BN
UK
Tel: +44 (0) 1993 848726
E-mail: info@chandospublishing.com
www.chandospublishing.com

Chandos Publishing is an imprint of Woodhead Publishing Limited

Woodhead Publishing Limited
Abington Hall
Granta Park
Great Abington
Cambridge CB21 6AH
UK
www.woodheadpublishing.com

First published in 2010

ISBN: 978 1 84334 578 7

© Richard J. Moniz Jr, 2010

British Library Cataloguing-in-Publication Data.
A catalogue record for this book is available from the British Library.

Assistant commissioning editor: Helen Brown

Typeset in the UK by Concerto.
Printed in the UK and USA.

Printed in the UK by 4edge Limited - www.4edge.co.uk

Contents

About the author

Dr Richard Moniz is the director of library services at Johnson & Wales University's Charlotte, NC, campus and an adjunct professor for the library and information studies program at the University of North Carolina at Greensboro. Prior to his current position, he served as the director of library services and head of information technology at Johnson & Wales University's North Miami campus. In addition to a master's degree in library and information studies from the University of Rhode Island, he holds a master's in history from Rhode Island College and a doctorate in education from Florida International University. He has taught undergraduate courses on world history, American government, an introduction to computers and microcomputer applications, as well as graduate courses in information sources and services and library administration and management. He has published in *Library Journal*, *North Carolina Libraries*, *College & Undergraduate Libraries* and *Library Leadership and Management*. He served as president of Metrolina Library Association in 2007 and currently serves on the American Library Association's Library Leadership and Management Association's Planning and Evaluating Library Services Committee and chairs its Continuing Education Committee. Dr Moniz has served on non-profit boards beyond these library-related posts, such as those of Carolina Raptor Center and the Charlotte Museum of History. He has been responsible for Johnson & Wales University's annual fundraising campaign for the Arts & Science Council, a local united arts fund in Charlotte. In other leadership-related experiences, he has completed the Arts & Science Council leadership training program and the Harvard University/Association of College and Research Libraries' leadership training program; other leadership training includes Stephen Covey's course on 'Seven Habits of Highly Effective Managers' and Bob Nelson's '1001 Ways to Reward Employees'. He is a recipient of Southeast Florida Library Information Network's Star Award as well as Johnson & Wales University's Special Recognition, Research and Community Service Awards. He lives in Charlotte with his wife and two boys, Kevin and Christopher, and can be reached by e-mail at richard.moniz@jwu.edu.

List of acronyms

ACRL	Association of College and Research Libraries
ALA	American Library Association
EI	emotional intelligence
HBCU	Historically Black Colleges and Universities
ITS	information technology services
JA	judge advocate
LLAMA	Library Leadership and Management Association
LPC	least preferred co-worker
MLIS	master's in library and information studies
OCP	organizational culture profile
SWOTs	strengths/weaknesses/opportunities/threats

Introduction

If in fact this is to be seen as a crash course in library management, I believe that I am uniquely qualified to be addressing you. This is not because I see myself as some super or ideal manager. I have many faults and continue to learn from my mistakes all the time (although hopefully those mistakes are a little less frequent than in the past). Rather, I tend to think I am at least a bit unusual and have something special I would like to share because of how I ended up here. Please bear with me as my story has relevance to our task at hand, the exploration of library management.

When I graduated with my master's in library and information studies degree in 1997, I had already completed several years of various library work. My experiences included spending three years in the technical services department at Rhode Island College's James P. Adams Library, a year in the audio/visual, periodicals and technical services departments at the University of Rhode Island (I basically went wherever I was needed at a given point in time), a short stint in the audio/visual department at the main branch of Madison Public Library (Wisconsin), a summer as an intern at the Smithsonian Institution (where, in fact, I was required to spend most of my time at the Library of Congress), a semester as an intern at the reference desk at James P. Adams Library and a semester as an intern at Coventry Public Library in Coventry, RI (where I helped organize their special collections). While this may sound impressive, you might also significantly note that none of these jobs was as a librarian but rather at the page, library assistant, etc., level. So when I subsequently applied for a job as an instruction librarian at Johnson & Wales University's Providence campus, I was taken completely by surprise when the dean of libraries called and asked me if I 'would like to head up the library at the Florida campus' instead. Despite the pride I had in my history degree, I subsequently discovered that I was hired largely because of my experience as a Windows 95 technical support engineer (a job I had held in Wisconsin just prior to going back to school for my MLIS). Essentially, the Florida campus needed someone who could also run its fledgling information technology services operations, and I met this unadvertised qualification.

None of this story so far is particularly funny or exciting, right? Well, this next part is where it gets a bit more interesting. I flew out to Florida for a brief visit prior to formally accepting the position. The library was being operated out of what was something like a classroom space, and would move into a newly built library under my supervision once I arrived to stay. I was able to spend part of one day with the former director, who would be gone by the time I arrived to take up residence. At the time there was only one other non-student employee (a library assistant who later went on to complete her MLIS). In my first month, I was told I would be able to hire another librarian, with more librarians to be added in successive years. When I finally arrived on campus, I found out that the dean and special assistant to the vice president (now the vice president and president of that campus, respectively) were not available. As a result, someone directed me to the maintenance shop. A gentleman from maintenance then walked me to the library, opened the door with his key (it was summer and the library was only open on a very limited basis for a few summer classes) and said, 'Well, I guess you know what to do so I am taking off.'

I told you there was a point, and I am getting to it. I found myself standing there not knowing where anything was, with no actual experience as a professional librarian and, as I was soon to realize, no library management experience whatsoever. Technically, I had exactly one month to oversee the move into the newly built library, hire a librarian, draft and/or review policies, set up a new computer lab, revamp the campus's old computer labs, etc. Needless to say, I practically lived at work for the remainder of the summer. Back then I knew so very little about what I am writing about in this book. But I am still getting just a little ahead of myself.

Fast-forward a number of years... Shortly after arriving in Charlotte, I completed a doctorate in education and was recruited by Dr Barbara Feldman to teach in the library science program for the University of North Carolina at Greensboro. While I have also taught the information sources and services course, my mainstay quickly became the library administration and management course. As I became more and more engrossed in the materials for the course and learned by trial and error what worked best and what didn't, I developed a more sophisticated philosophy with regard to understanding library administration. In fact, I started conducting research on this very thing and began thinking to an even greater extent about the experiences I had lived through in my 12 years as a director of library services with Johnson & Wales University. This was a very exciting time, as I felt I had turned a corner. Many librarians had helped me along the way, and now it was my turn to help others as well.

My experience and my research have led me to believe that there are several key ingredients to teaching library administration to library science students, and ultimately to becoming an effective library administrator. Put succinctly, one should have some understanding of management theory, a good sense of one's own strengths and weaknesses as a manager, an understanding of the staff as individuals, an ability to problem-solve and some tools for doing so, an understanding of one's organizational culture, and experience. A couple of points need to be expanded upon here. I believe that good management and good teaching and learning have much in common. In the workplace great discussions have led to better library services, and better classroom discussion has led to better exploration of problems and issues. To my staff and my students, I owe a great deal. I learn from both all the time. One of the most effective means of fostering discussion in the classroom is through case studies (ideally pulled from the kinds of issues that my staff and I face in 'real life'), and that is why some are included here. Another point I would like to make is relative to experience. If I had a dollar for every time I've heard a staff member or student say 'I have no experience with management', I would undoubtedly be rich. After hearing this statement, I almost invariably find out that the staff member or student worked as an event planner for several years, managed all of their family's activities and finances, worked in a law firm helping coordinate various activities, etc. My point is that nobody comes with a blank slate, and these previous experiences do count.

As I usually do with my students, I have shared with you here my experience and philosophy to some extent. I have a couple more orders of business before we begin on the formal journey. I always explain to my students the following points... I work as the director of library services for Johnson & Wales University in Charlotte, NC, a private, not-for-profit institution of higher education that has approximately 2,500 students studying in three programs (culinary arts, business and hospitality). We are part of a broader Johnson & Wales University system of 15,000 students. My staff consist of five librarians: three full-time and two part-time. While I will guard as much as I can against it, I may suggest or imply that 'this is the way it should be done' when, in fact, what I am really saying (without realizing it) is 'this is the way I believe it should be done at a Johnson & Wales branch campus'. This, to me, is the conundrum of having experience, especially if the bulk of it comes, as does mine, from a given organization. As stated earlier, and as will be made clear in this text, decisions are made within the context of an organizational culture. Sometimes these decisions would readily transfer to being good decisions in other organizations, and sometimes they could constitute the worst possible approach to take. As we go forward, I remind you as I would my class that I am merely a facilitator or guide. I do not have a crystal ball, and you should feel free to question me and my assumptions wherever they might arise.

On a last note, it is pertinent to discuss how this book is organized. Throughout each chapter an attempt has been made to connect and lay bare some of the potential relevance and application of theories and concepts to the world of a library manager. Chapter 1 explores influential historical, as well as some more recent, general management theories and thoughts. Chapter 2 is focused on getting to know oneself better as a person, manager and leader. Chapter 3 examines the all-important issue in any workplace: motivation. Chapter 4 explores issues related to organizational culture and workplace socialization. Chapter 5 involves a discussion on the broad issue of communication. Lastly, Chapter 6 targets issues related to decision-making and effective leadership. It should be noted that any organization that one would come up with is in truth an artificial one. That is, all of these concepts are very much interrelated. To be an effective library manager, one needs to understand how to apply theory, one's own strengths and weaknesses, how people are motivated, how aspects of culture affect behavior and decision-making, how decision-making can be flawed and how to communicate with and lead others. These skills and abilities need to be integrated into one's understanding of behavior on a day-to-day and moment-to-moment basis.

One other note on organization is relevant. This book is intended to be employed either as a textbook for a course on library administration or for a practicing librarian who is stepping into a role as a library manager. As such, each chapter has questions for discussion or consideration. Each also has a relevant case study with associated questions and some project ideas for applying the material in the chapter or exploring it in new and different ways. It is my hope that, after having read and reflected on the content presented here, when someone hands you the keys to the library and says 'well, I guess you know what to do so I am taking off', you will, in fact, know what to do!

History of managerial thought: a brief overview

The history of management is typically broken down into schools of thought and resultant theories. Rather than serving as a comprehensive review, this chapter is intended to provide you with a general overview of some of the theory which has emerged. While not all aspects of the various schools and theories are equally applicable to managing in the library environment, each perspective can help layer one's understanding of given situations and problems.

Frederick Winslow Taylor and scientific management

Almost to a fault, books on management and organizational behavior begin with a discussion of the work of Frederick Winslow Taylor and his seminal book originally published in 1911, *The Principles of Scientific Management*. According to Taylor, the 'best management is a true science' (Taylor, [1911] 1947: 7). He went on to outline his principles, which he referred to as scientific management. While his studies focused primarily on industrial labor, such as workers in the Midvale and Bethlehem Steel companies, he actually intended his principles to apply to all environments, even non-profits. Taylor's idea was to focus on creating ever-greater efficiencies by carefully studying the work that needed to be done and finding a way to maximize the labor of workers. In his somewhat tortured prose:

> The enormous saving of time and therefore increase in output which it is possible to effect through eliminating unnecessary

motions and substituting fast for slow and inefficient motions for the men working in our trades can be fully realized only after one has personally seen the improvement which rests from a thorough motion and time study... (Ibid.: 24)

There is a slightly disturbing level of paternalism embedded in his book, as he refers to a common worker lacking education as being 'so stupid that the word "percentage" has no meaning to him, and he must consequently be trained by a more intelligent man than himself' (ibid.: 59). Still, his work stands as a foundational piece on modern management, especially due to the fact that his approach achieved measurable results.

Later in his career, at a bicycle ball factory, he was able to move the plant in the direction of much greater efficiencies by applying his principles. Just how much greater was production due to his efforts? By the time he was done, 35 women were doing the work of 120 and making twice the wages. It should be noted on this latter point that he felt greater efficiencies should lead to better pay for the workers (although he gave very little by way of advice on how the workers would be able to protect these higher wages in the long run). Also, in creating the efficiencies it was ultimately discovered that the women were more productive working an 8.5-hour as opposed to a 10.5-hour shift and if they were actually *required* to take breaks at specific intervals.

For most librarians, the concept of library work as something that can be made brutally efficient is probably not just foreign but repugnant. Indeed, when one thinks of Taylor's work, there seem to be some warnings there as well. Taylor said at the outset of his book that 'In the past the man has been first, in the future the system must be first' (ibid.: 7). Hardly any of us would agree on this overly brash statement, which would seem to regard library staff as cogs in a machine. That said, as we push into the twenty-first century a number of changes have occurred that oblige us to pay greater attention to efficiencies. The most obvious, of course, is the ubiquitous nature of the internet and electronic resources. To some extent this has created competition for the provision of information resources and services which hadn't existed before. More significantly, since the financial crisis beginning in 2008 libraries have almost universally had budgets slashed. One need not adhere exclusively to Taylor's approach to and emphasis on efficiency to recognize benefits towards applying it on a *limited* basis to collections management, staffing and other areas.

For example, initial budget cuts in 2009 forced the library staff at Johnson & Wales University's Charlotte campus to consider the possibility of future cuts as well. One line item explored was the periodicals collection. Many of the print periodicals by this time were getting very little use. By compiling a list of titles that were available electronically through databases, it was possible to narrow down potential titles with overlap. Since the titles were available to students and faculty in electronic format, the physical subscriptions could be cut. This approach would need to be discussed with the faculty and wouldn't be without its negative consequences, not least of which would be the lack of ability to browse the titles or periodicals themselves physically. With all of these concerns acknowledged, however, when faced with a choice between cutting overlapped print titles and losing staff positions or other collection development funds, a focus on efficiency in one area can lead to benefits in others. Numerous other examples of efficiencies could be presented here but, on a last note, it should almost go without saying that new technologies frequently offer the opportunity for not just greater efficiencies but also enhanced services in the modern library.

Max Weber and bureaucratic management

In addition to the concept of brutal efficiencies, another 'nasty word' for librarians and most people in general is bureaucracy. As we move into the twenty-first century, a bureaucratic approach to management has all sorts of negative connotations. We have a tendency to conjure up some huge pile of paperwork that we need to fill out for a simple request or think of waiting in a long line at the Department of Motor Vehicles. Credited largely to its description by Max Weber in the early twentieth century, the idea of a bureaucracy was a leap forward at the time. Weber's belief in a highly structured and rational approach has been said to have grown out of his experience in the German army (Bennis, 1961). He described his concept of a bureaucracy, among other places, in his book *Economy and Society*. According to Weber, 'Experience tends universally to show that the purely bureaucratic type of organization… is, from a purely technical point of view, capable of attaining the highest degree of efficiency and is in this sense formally the most rational known means of exercising authority over human beings.' He expands upon his idea by discussing the need for 'rational administration by trained specialized officials' (Weber, [1922] 1978: 997). Clearly, there are advantages to his view, which sought to encourage organizations to consider very carefully their needs and how they were constructed to meet those needs. His overwhelming emphasis is on structure and specialization. Perhaps its greatest weakness is the fact that this view neglects the somewhat irrational or psychological aspects of organizations, which, as they are made up of individuals, are a factor in need of consideration when running any enterprise.

As residents of the twenty-first century and once again making reference to the complicated mix of entanglements which led to the economic downturn in 2008 and 2009, structures are important. Understanding how things fit together, whether they are real estate companies or banks, departments within a given organization or reporting lines within a department, is critical. What Weber did was to codify the need for assigning responsibilities and accountability in a highly logical manner. There is clear relevance here for libraries. While organizational culture will be discussed in detail in a later chapter, it should be noted here that the culture of an organization or library determines its effectiveness, and this, in turn, is significantly affected by its associated reporting lines, policies and procedures. This is not a bad thing. It just means that managers need to be cognizant not only of the bureaucracy as it exists, but also in considering how effective it is in furthering the mission of the organization. Again, it is appropriate to relate the accountability aspect of this theory to the mission of libraries in the educational environment being more and more focused on specific outcomes, specifically learning outcomes. Thus systems, policies and structure need to be aligned to produce the expected results. Lastly, while there is often much overlap, a significant amount of library work requires specialization – in the areas of cataloging and systems, for example.

A couple of my experiences might help relate this issue further as to how, in particular, this might apply especially in growing organizations. Shortly after opening a new campus library for Johnson & Wales University, I discussed with the vice president my plans to communicate with the various academic departments through assigned library liaisons. He suggested that we consider creating a very formal library committee, since, in his words, 'We will someday be bigger and your less formal structure and approach may prove less effective.' I decided to do just that, creating a committee that had functional representation from all library areas as well as all faculty departments. It later also grew to include student, ITS and career development representatives. It has been an effective committee which has met regularly over several years as the campus has grown from 1,000 to 2,500 students. On another point, while the Johnson & Wales' Charlotte campus library's organizational chart is as flat as could be in terms of bureaucracy, individual librarians are given specific mandates to lead in certain areas. With cataloging/collection management, reference services and information literacy instruction all relating to core aspects of the mission, each of these areas has a clearly assigned leader.

Henri Fayol and the five functions of management

Frenchman Henri Fayol, while a contemporary of Weber, became more widely known long after his death. He published the book *General and Industrial Management* in 1916, but it was not translated into English until many years later. According to one author who recently updated and revised Fayol's text, 'Fayol was the first author to 1) identify management as a process, 2) break that process down into a series of subparts, and 3) lay out a series of principles by which management could apply the process to make best use of the organization's personnel' (Fayol, [1916] 1984: 7). In one sense, while Weber highlighted the importance of structure to the actual job of managing, Fayol was the first to structure how we think about management itself. More specifically, he identified what he considered to be the five functions of management and the 14 principles of management. The latter were as follows (ibid.: 61–2):

- division of work
- authority and responsibility
- discipline
- unity of command
- unity of direction
- subordination of the individual's interests to the general interest
- remuneration of personnel
- centralization
- scalar chain (line of authority)
- order

- equity
- stability of tenure of personnel
- initiative
- *ésprit de corps.*

The five functions mentioned above were planning, organizing, coordinating, commanding and controlling. These functions have no need for citation as they are widely considered to be common knowledge. Indeed, many textbooks on management even today are organized based on this very scheme. It is worth briefly noting each of these functions and commenting on some ways in which they might apply specifically to library management.

Planning is a process necessary for all libraries. According to Fayol, a plan consists of many elements, some of which include unity, flexibility and awareness of trends (ibid.). In the academic library environment, one aspect of unity is that the library's plan should align and take direction from the university or college's plan. It can't be overstated how important this is. For the library staff to achieve their shared goals, they need to make this connection explicit. Flexibility is another very relevant concept to planning for libraries today. With the ever-greater reliance on new technologies, one needs to consider a plan that will incorporate new possibilities (e.g. who could have predicted the impact of blogs, wikis, social networking etc. ten years ago?). An awareness of trends is also critical. This can be accomplished through networking, keeping up on library literature and attending conferences. I have also found my staff to be a great source as well. Lastly, one final note, planning should involve the entire library staff for two primary reasons: participation will lead to commitment and to better ideas overall.

Organizing is another key element highlighted by Fayol. He felt that it was important to have a clear organizational chart and be good at selecting personnel. Managers should delegate, but not entirely 'divorce themselves from the details' (ibid.: 43). Having a clear organizational chart and knowing which people to plug in are critical in any library. Hiring is a very important, if not the most important, function of a manager and a topic one should explore further (i.e. beyond this book). The two most important points that can be made here, however, are that you should always seek smart employees and you need to pay careful attention to organizational fit. The first point may seem self-evident, but many insecure managers tend to hire people of lesser quality for fear that they will outshine them. Experience has indicated that, quite the contrary, hiring high-aptitude employees raises the image and cachet of not just the manager but the entire library staff. Additionally, one of the worst hires one can make is a very bright person who is an exceptionally poor organizational fit. Be sure to consider both the positive and potentially negative aspects of your library's culture from an outside perspective, and then ask whether or not this person will be able to adjust.

Coordinating is yet another key function. Taking Fayol's negatives on this point and turning them around, success in this area can be seen by a wide degree of cooperation in the organization. Library staff do not just understand their role, but appreciate the role of the other library staff and understand how they all fit together to accomplish the library's mission. Communication by the manager is a key element here. Managers need to hold meetings and set agendas that highlight these key pieces. In an academic library environment, there is also a relationship across the campus that is critical. Many campuses hold department head or equivalent meetings on a monthly basis, at which time the library director and other key department heads have a chance to share information and look for opportunities to cooperate for the benefit of the institution.

Commanding, according to Fayol (ibid.), involves a number of elements such as knowing your staff, dealing with incompetent staff and balancing the personal needs of staff with those of the organization. The importance of knowing your staff as individuals can't be overstated. I would find it hard to believe that a manager who completely fails in this area could be successful (more on this in the chapter on motivation). In handling incompetence, one needs to proceed with caution and forethought. It is important to do your job as a manager, which includes helping staff who are not living up to expectations. They are not simply to be written off, but should receive attention focused on specific problems they are having. It is very important not to make assumptions but first to listen to an employee who is having problems to find out where they originate and what can be done. If it goes further, you should begin to document discussions and give notice of problems in writing to an employee before terminating. No matter how bad the behavior or failure of the employee, this last task is especially difficult. It is probably the hardest aspect of being a library manager. Balancing the needs of staff and organization is difficult as well. Some library managers lean distinctly in one direction or the other. When making decisions, however, it is possible to weigh both by considering not just short-term but the long-term needs of both. This is true even if the long-term health and needs of both ultimately require a separation of the employee from the library.

Lastly, controlling is the function, according to Fayol (ibid.), which concerns issues such as budget and outcomes. A library manager needs to be able to monitor expenditures carefully, as would be expected in any organization with a budget. For many academic libraries, the two biggest line items in this regard are salaries and collection development funds. In some cases, a library manager may apportion responsibility for managing parts of the latter to other library staff but remain responsible for the overall figures. Also peculiar to the circumstances of any academic library is the need to focus on both customer service and student learning outcomes. The former would be very important to any public library and the latter to any school library as well. It is also critical to measure the effectiveness of library services, and in turn to make sure that you are measuring the right things on a regular basis. This is often done through surveys, testing, statistics, focus groups, etc.

Elton Mayo and the Hawthorne studies

Following the scientific school of management thought was the behavioral school. The development of its theories owed a great deal to the discipline of psychology and grew out of a greater concern for the individual worker or groups of workers. The writings of Elton Mayo and others formed the base from which this approach grew. Mayo's most significant contribution was in popularizing the results of the Hawthorne studies. While the 'Hawthorne effect' is actually a common term served up as a warning that participants in a study, by their very awareness of being studied, may behave differently, the studies at the Hawthorne plant had a significant positive impact on our understanding of how important aspects of psychology are to managerial theory and practice.

While there were four studies conducted between 1927 and 1932, including somewhat famous interview and illumination studies, the most critical was a study involving workers who assembled telephone wire relays. The goal of the research was to improve production by introducing various alterations to the way work was done. According to Mayo, six women were chosen from the plant's 'operatives' to work in a separate room since 'it was believed that such changes were more likely to be noticed by the official observers if the group was small' (Mayo, [1933] 1960: 55). In all, more than a dozen different changes were introduced over time, including changing the piece rate such that the smaller group was judged together (and paid according to group output), introducing specific rest periods varying in number and duration, providing refreshments and allowing workers to work a shorter shift. Mayo noted:

> Before every change of program, the group is consulted. Their comments are listened to and discussed; sometimes their objections are allowed to negative a suggestion. The group unquestionably develops a sense of participation in the critical determinations and becomes something of a social unit. (Ibid.: 69)

Mayo goes on to add:

> The company, in the interest of developing a new form of scientific control... incidentally altered the total pattern... The consequence was that there was a period during which the individual workers and the group had to re-adapt themselves to... a milieu in which their own self-determination and their social well-being ranked first and the work was incidental. (Ibid.: 70–1)

This last statement is most illuminating. While the researchers had set out to discover what conditions were best for production, they inadvertently discovered something more profound. Concern for workers by management, allowing employees to have input in procedures and policies and having a close-knit team led to not just a better work environment but enhanced production.

While the experiments at the Hawthorne plant and the validity of the results have been much debated and discussed over the years, there can be no doubt that, at the very least, they had stumbled upon something important which relates directly to libraries. Much more will be said about teamwork and fostering communication in later chapters. The work of Mayo, however, is critical in pointing out that a manager needs to be concerned about the welfare of his or her employees, should involve library staff in making decisions about how their work is to be done whenever possible and should do his or her best to encourage camaraderie among the group.

Doug McGregor and Theory X and Theory Y

Another seminal figure in the history of managerial thought is Doug McGregor. While he spoke and wrote about the topic on a number of occasions, his book *The Human Side of Enterprise* was a groundbreaking thesis on what has been referred to as 'Theory X and Theory Y' management. McGregor (1960) emphasized that all managers have an innate theory that they apply to managing people, whether they recognize it or not. These theories lead them, in turn, to make a series of assumptions from which they proceed actually to manage. According to Theory X, which McGregor asserts most managers adhere to, people are basically lazy, will avoid work and need to be told what to do. He believed that this theory was simply a way for management to abrogate responsibility for poor performance. He posited that a Theory Y approach would be not just more conscientious, but also more productive. While lengthy it is worth quoting its associated assumptions:

1. The expenditure of physical and mental effort in work is as natural as play or rest...

2. External control and the threat of punishment are not the only means for bringing about effort toward organizational objectives. Man will exercise self-direction and self-control in the service of objectives to which he is committed...

3. Commitment to objectives is a function of the rewards associated with the achievement...

4. The average human being learns, under proper conditions, not only to accept but to seek responsibility...

5. The capacity to exercise a relatively high degree of imagination, ingenuity, and creativity in the solution of organizational problems is widely, not narrowly, distributed in the population...

6. Under the conditions of modern industrial life, the intellectual potentialities of the average human being are only partially utilized... (Ibid.: 47–8)

There are some obvious implications in these assumptions for issues such as motivating employees, and perhaps somewhat less obvious implications with regard to decision-making which will be addressed in future chapters. For now, however, a general connection needs to be drawn as to what this means for a library administrator.

While many people would see the above assumptions as self-evident, many would not. Groundbreaking in its day, application of the Theory Y concept is still often lacking in practice, due to the difference which usually exists between what people espouse and what they actually do. Chris Argyris (2002) has laid out the case in great detail that, under normal conditions, most people do not see the incongruity between what he labels theories-in-use versus espoused theories. That is, we hear a manager speak from one perspective and then act from another. For example, the library world is not exempt from stories of managers who talk about fostering open communication only to insult it blatantly or more subtly discourage it. Oftentimes this comes from a place whereby a manager espouses a belief in Theory Y, but deep down does not trust it or his employees and thus acts on Theory X assumptions. The temptation to abandon a Theory Y approach can be particularly alluring after having an employee fail repeatedly at a task. There is then a tendency to want just to step in and do the job oneself. The worst danger, of course, would be to transfer the experience by then making wrong assumptions about staff in general and following this up with managerial decisions based on those assumptions. A library manager must believe in his or her staff and do what he or she can to manage them based on the assumption that deep down the employee does want to do his or her job well. As an administrator, it is necessary to have an ongoing conversation with individual staff about the library's goals and the employee's personal goals. While this will be discussed further in the chapter on motivation, it should be noted that this is an area where a 'Tayloresque' strict adherence to efficiencies can sometimes be at odds with productivity. A focus on personal goals may not always seem to be getting the organization from point A to point B by the most direct route, but paying attention to the individual's needs and drives can often allow you to achieve the organization's objectives with a much greater degree of quality. One would be surprised and sometimes even amazed as to how many fantastic ideas may come from staff working to a large extent at their own self-direction and on projects of great personal importance *to them.*

Kurt Lewin and open systems theory

Another approach, developed by Kurt Lewin and which gained adherents in the latter half of the twentieth century, is open systems theory. Like Weber, Lewin was a much bigger figure in the sense that his impact extended far beyond management. In articles such as 'Frontiers in group dynamics: concept, method and reality in social science; social equilibria and social change', published in 1947, he established some of the basic methods by which research is conducted in the social sciences today. For our purposes here, however, Lewin's open system focused on problems by 'emphasizing interdependency, complex causality, the whole being different than the sum of its parts and the need to deal with organized patterns or wholes' (Wolf, 1973: 323). After first establishing his broader theoretical framework (often referred to as a theory of a theory or metatheory), which will not be discussed here, Lewin was then able to theorize further that leadership style had a direct impact on group performance and participation in groups also had an effect on overall group performance. He was ultimately able to show that a democratic style of leadership had the greatest long-term benefits in terms of productivity, and that participation in the decision-making process by workers also led to significant increases in productivity. In the words of management guru Stephen Covey (1997: 26), 'When people are involved in the problem, they become increasingly committed to coming up with solutions to the problem.'

Lewin's work offers some profound insight and relevance into the management of libraries. All libraries tend to be more productive under some level of democratic leadership and greater staff participation in the decision-making process, especially in the case of academic libraries. Academia in general is built on the premise that education and learning should involve an ongoing conversation and, as such, this model fits nicely. Lewin's description of interdependence also has special relevance in that academic libraries are part of a broader institutional framework that includes faculty, students and other departmental units, as well as the bigger environment of state, country, etc. There can be no doubt that all of these entities are connected, and that library decisions are both affected by and have an effect upon them. Thus when making decisions we often do environmental scans, looking carefully at broad national and regional trends as well as soliciting feedback and concerns on a regular basis from important constituents such as students and faculty. In fact, assessment of this type is critical for success. Furthermore, in all libraries the recognition of interdependence also suggests a need to consider the library from a political perspective. Who needs to be aware of the value of the library (e.g. the principal, the dean, the community, etc.)? How can the library be more effective by partnering with other departments (e.g. perhaps by working with ITS on computer-related information literacy components in an academic library, or in a public library by hosting information on job hunting and researching with a local government employment agency)?

While not all decisions can be made democratically, most meaningful decisions can either be discussed with staff or broken down into viable options for discussion. It is almost universally true that by involving library staff in decision-making, not only do you gain greater long-term commitment, as Lewin found, but as stated earlier you also get significantly better decisions overall. This will be discussed further in the chapter on decision-making. In concluding our consideration of open systems theory, however, it is sufficient to say that one needs to consider how to involve staff appropriately in decision-making, and the interconnectedness of the library with other areas.

Contingency theories

Contingency theories, or the contingency approach to management, are multifaceted and have many implications. For now, however, it will suffice to provide an overview and some relevant highlights. Contingency theories, in a sense, question the universal applicability implied by some of the theories already discussed (although they do more readily relate to Lewin's open system concept). In a nutshell, contingency theories posit that good management will look different based on situational variables. Early research on contingency theory points out that such variables as style of leadership, job design, participation in decision-making and organizational structure are critical to understanding what will lead to a good overall managerial outcome (Shepard and Hougland, 1978: 414). A more recent definition of contingency theories in the *Encyclopedia of Management* breaks them down into two categories: environmental contingencies and internal contingencies (Helms, 2000: 125–6).

Environmental contingency theories focus mainly on the relative stability of the environment. In relation to libraries, as has already been mentioned, change is occurring at a rapid pace, leading to a significant degree of instability. This alone seems to suggest an emphasis on flexibility. Internal contingencies concern factors such as the size of an organization. A larger library with more staff will have to be managed differently and probably require more formality, for example, all other factors being equal, than a library with fewer staff. The types of employees in an organization also play a role here within the internal contingency context. Managing librarians with MLIS degrees and a wide range of experience is going to be different to managing high-school students working part-time at McDonalds. Again, if flexibility is required due to the external situation libraries face, an appreciation of and ability to utilize highly educated staff fully are relevant to the internal situation.

One of the more interesting theorists within the many in this area is Fred Fiedler. Fiedler is known for an instrument referred to as the LPC or 'least preferred co-worker'. A manager who takes this test is asked to rate their least preferred associate on a whole number of different characteristics. Once tallied, the results indicate whether or not the individual is task or relationship oriented. Further study has shown that a task orientation to management, which focuses almost exclusively on what needs to get done as opposed to the individual employees, is most effective at the polar extremes whereby a manager has a very high or very low degree of power and group cohesion. The relationship approach, focused as one would expect on the individual relationship with employees, works better in more moderate circumstances (Fiedler, 1964).

Robert Greenleaf and servant leadership

You might ask yourself why a section here is dedicated to servant leadership. After all, isn't that what Chapter 6 is all about? Aren't we discussing management theory? The answer is that, much like many of the authors mentioned in this text, Greenleaf's work extends across the topics we will be exploring. In his book *On Becoming a Servant Leader*, Greenleaf (1996) conveys his overall theory of management. Unlike Fayol's five functions of management, Greenleaf has subsumed them into three areas: planning, deciding and communicating. We started with Taylor's view, which, as you may recall, gives primacy to the system. Greenleaf is the polar opposite. According to Greenleaf, 'the work exists for the person as much as the person exists for the work' (ibid.: 117). An ideal manager should not rely on coercion, but rather persuasion as much as possible. In this highly people-centered philosophy, a manager should be able to say, 'I am in the business of growing people – people who are stronger, healthier, more autonomous, more self-reliant, more competent' (ibid.: 122). Greenleaf restates this later with an emphasis placed specifically on service: 'It is more important to use one's power affirmatively to serve, in the sense that those being served, while being served, become healthier, wiser, freer, more autonomous, and more likely themselves to become servants' (ibid.: 171).

In the role of library director or manager, one is responsible for both the people who report to you and the overall mission. One of the best-kept secrets of the business world is that employees who are treated a certain way will then turn around and treat the customers accordingly. While a library manager must set an agenda and lead, he or she must also be willing to serve. By serving one is not just referring to one's supervisor or the institution. In order to help direct subordinates achieve their potential, good managers will also look for ways to serve their employees. Oftentimes library staff have great ideas and initiatives, but need someone to help clear a path or allocate resources. Make no mistake about it, a library administrator is there to serve staff and to encourage success both in their careers and in furthering the library's mission. In the words of Filippa Anzalone (2007: 809), who writes about applying servant leadership in a law library, 'The leader serves as the fulcrum of the pyramid, at its base, guiding the organization by serving the employees and making sure that they have the proper resources to do their jobs.'

Conclusion

In conclusion, a note of wisdom from the preface to a translated edition of Henri Fayol's *General and Industrial Management* is especially pertinent. The author states that 'people tend to revert, unless specially trained to do otherwise, to one school of thought on which to base their decisions, the one through which they have developed their careers and which they find most familiar, comfortable and secure. Such one-dimensional thinking is the hallmark of the mediocre manager...' (Gray in Fayol, [1916] 1984: 4). Such advice seems even more pertinent to the experienced manager than to the beginner, and is applicable beyond decision-making to management as a whole. One should not simply pick one's favorite of the above theories and move on, but seek to understand each of them (and others) and weigh their value in given situations. For library managers, it should also be added that we too often look only within our profession; that is, we examine what other library managers are doing. Significant insight and creativity can be achieved by exploring management in other contexts as well.

Thoughts for consideration or discussion

- In your opinion, what aspects of library services lend themselves to a Taylorist approach? That is, how should academic, public and school libraries seek to achieve efficiencies?

- What does the organizational chart look like in the library you work in or in the local academic, public and/or school library? What does this structure say about the organization and its focus?

- What kind of plan and/or planning process is in place at your library, or what kinds of information can you discover about the planning process at various libraries directly on the internet or through articles in library journals and trade publications?

- Can you think of circumstances where it would be difficult to weigh the interests of individual staff against those of the institution? How do you manage in these circumstances?

- How would a Theory Y mentality change the way you would approach an employee who is not performing well in some areas?

- If a library exists in an open system, what kinds of interdependencies exist in academic libraries? In public libraries? In school libraries?

- How might the library and managing it be affected by the outside environment? What are the biggest environmental challenges that library staff face?

- Have you ever experienced or practiced managing according to the principles of servant leadership? If so, how?

Case study: Diane takes on a challenge

Diane recently took a position as library director at Venerable Old University, a private, highly selective liberal arts college with an enrollment of 2,000 undergraduate and 300 graduate students. Having worked at a similar, although slightly larger, private university for ten years, Diane had experience of three years in technical services and seven years in the reference department (with four years as the head of reference). She believes very strongly in information literacy, and took the job because, throughout the interviewing process, the search committee was adamant that they needed to do better in this area.

After six months on the job and having had the opportunity to get to know most of her staff of seven librarians fairly well, in addition to other department heads on campus, she was ready to start working towards some changes. In a recent meeting with the dean (who she reports to), she was encouraged to push forward with enhancing information literacy initiatives. In a separate meeting with the president, he reiterated this encouragement but added, 'Be sure you can make it happen with the staff you have. In fact, you should be able to do it with less as significant budget cuts are to be expected overall in the next couple of years.'

Of the seven full-time librarians, two worked in technical services (with neither serving as head of the department and both reporting directly to the director) and both seemed as though they had a fairly steady flow of work. That said, Diane noted to herself that the generous collection development funds might be one of the first things to go once the budget gets cut and this might mean less materials requiring processing. Four additional librarians were dedicated to reference, with one of these librarians serving as head of that area. The other full-time librarian did some reference work but focused mainly on library instruction (which was very basic and was based on a limited number of requests from faculty). This librarian reported to the head of reference. In terms of competence and tenure, most staff had been with Venerable Old University for 12 years or more. There was a mix of traditional skills and high levels of competence in most areas, yet the staff seemed 'dated'. There was very little going on in terms of professional development, conference attendance or publishing. When she asked around, Diane discovered that the previous library director was 'pretty much the only one engaged in these kinds of activities and even she had not done much in her last few years'.

She sat down thinking about the situation, and pulled up the library's last two strategic plans (one dated for the past five years and the other for the five years before that). As she perused them, she realized that the plans were identical in every way! She decided to ask around as to how the library staff put the plan together, and the common response was 'Plan? What plan? The old library director did all that herself. Besides, we all know our jobs anyway.' Diane went back to her desk, brought up her e-mail and scheduled a staff meeting for the following week.

- What kinds of challenges does Diane seem to face in moving forward?
- How does the structure of the staff lend itself to what she and the administration seem to view as the future of the library?
- How aware do the staff appear relative to the outside environment?
- How should she create a new plan? What would the first steps look like? What kinds of things might she need to be careful about?
- How do other departments fit into this, especially regarding information literacy? What other kinds of interdependencies might exist? How could these areas be approached?
- Can she take on all of these things at once? If she prioritizes, what comes first?
- What does the meeting agenda for the following week look like?

Project ideas

- Search a database containing academic journals for three articles relating to original research conducted based on one of the theories or ideas mentioned above. Write a paper/article that summarizes the research, relating it to how relevant the findings may be for a specific type of library or library environment.
- Further compare and contrast two of the theories related in this chapter.

2

Psychology and knowing oneself: how do these affect management and decision-making?

It almost goes without saying that each of us comes into library work with different strengths and weaknesses. We also come into library work with a multiplicity of different experiences and worldviews. There are a number of factors that go into making a manager successful. That said, understanding who you are from a variety of perspectives can help you become more effective as a manager. Indeed, one of the chapters in Daniel Goleman's book on emotional intelligence, which is discussed below, is entitled 'Know thyself' (Goleman, 1997: 46) It should be emphasized, however, that none of the approaches discussed below in and of itself will give you all the information that you need. They also don't give you an 'answer' *per se*. All they can do when taken together is to give you a more complete picture of who you are that, with discipline, you can use to your advantage in improving your managerial skills.

General personality tests

I often start my classes by asking the students to take one or more personality tests. There is always a mix of opinion on these, and when we open up the results for in-class and online discussion, a lively debate usually ensues. While any number of tests could be used and any number of qualities explored, a couple from *The Psychologist's Book of Personality Tests* by Louis Janda (2001) stand out as being particularly relevant. One is a test on assertiveness (provided below), and another is focused on empathy.

Before discussing the quality of assertiveness and how it applies, it is worth taking a moment to complete the following exercise to see just where you fall.

Assertiveness inventory for adults

The following inventory (printed with the permission of the original author, Dr John Galassi) is designed to provide information about the way in which you express yourself. Please answer the questions by writing a number from 0 to 4 in the space to the left of each item. Your answer should indicate how you generally express yourself in a variety of situations. If a particular situation does not apply to you, answer as you think you ought to act or how you would like to act. Do not deliberate over any individual question. Your first response to the question is probably your most accurate one.

0 = Almost always or always
1 = Usually
2 = Sometimes
3 = Seldom
4 = Never or rarely

_____ 1. Do you ignore it when someone pushes in front of you in line?

_____ 2. Do you find it difficult to ask a friend to do a favor for you?

_____ 3. If your boss or supervisor makes what you consider an unreasonable request, do you have difficulty saying no?

_____ 4. Are you reluctant to speak to an attractive acquaintance of the opposite sex?

_____ 5. Is it difficult for you to refuse unreasonable requests from your parents?

_____ 6. Do you find it difficult to accept compliments from your boss or supervisor?

_____ 7. Do you express your negative feelings to others when it is appropriate?

_____ 8. Do you freely volunteer information or opinions in discussions with people whom you do not know well?

_____ 9. If there was a public figure whom you greatly admired and respected at a large social gathering, would you make an effort to introduce yourself?

_____ 10. How often do you openly express justified feelings of anger to your parents?

_____ 11. If you have a friend of whom your parents do not approve, do you make an effort to help them get to know one another better?

_____ 12. If you were watching a TV program in which you were very interested and a close relative was disturbing you, would you ask them to be quiet?

_____ 13. Do you play an important part in deciding how you and your close friends spend your leisure time together?

_____ 14. If you are angry at your spouse, boyfriend, girlfriend, is it difficult for you to tell him/her?

_____ 15. If a friend who is supposed to pick you up for an important engagement calls 15 minutes before he/she is supposed to be there and says that he/she cannot make it, do you express your annoyance?

_____ 16. If in a rush you stop by a supermarket to pick up a few items, would you ask to go before someone in the checkout line?

_____ 17. Do you find it difficult to refuse the requests of others?

_____ 18. If your boss or supervisor expresses opinions with which you strongly disagree, do you venture to state your own point of view?

_____ 19. If you have a close friend whom your spouse, boyfriend, girlfriend dislikes and constantly criticizes, would you inform him/her that you disagree and tell him/her of your friend's assets?

_____ 20. Do you find it difficult to ask favors of others?

_____ 21. If food which is not to your satisfaction was served in a good restaurant, would you bring it to the waiter's attention?

_____ 22. Do you tend to drag out your apologies?

_____ 23. When necessary, do you find it difficult to ask favors of your parents?

_____ 24. Do you insist that others do their fair share of the work?

_____ 25. Do you have difficulty saying no to salesmen?

_____ 26. Are you reluctant to speak up in a discussion with a small group of friends?

_____ 27. Do you express anger or annoyance to your boss or supervisor when it is justified?

_____ 28. Do you compliment and praise others?

_____ 29. Do you have difficulty asking a close friend to do an important favor, even though it will cause him/her some inconvenience?

_____ 30. If a close relative makes what you consider to be an unreasonable request, do you have difficulty saying no?

_____ 31. If your boss or supervisor makes a statement that you consider untrue, do you question it aloud?

_____ 32. If you find yourself becoming fond of a friend, do you have difficulty expressing these feelings to that person?

_____ 33. Do you have difficulty exchanging a purchase with which you are dissatisfied?

_____ 34. If someone in authority interrupts you in the middle of an important conversation, do you request that the person wait until you have finished?

_____ 35. If a person of the opposite sex whom you have been wanting to meet directs attention to you at a party, do you take the initiative in beginning the conversation?

_____ 36. Do you hesitate to express resentment to a friend who has unjustifiably criticized you?

_____ 37. If your parents wanted you to come home for a weekend visit and you had made important plans, would you change your plans?

_____ 38. Are you reluctant to speak up in a discussion or debate?

_____ 39. If a friend who has borrowed $5.00 from you seems to have forgotten about it, is it difficult for you to remind this person?

_____ 40. If your boss or supervisor teases you to the point that it is no longer fun, do you have difficulty expressing your displeasure?

_____ 41. If your spouse, boyfriend, girlfriend is blatantly unfair, do you find it difficult to say something about it to him/her?

_____ 42. If a clerk in a store waits on someone who has come in after you when you are in a rush, do you call his attention to the matter?

____ 43. If you lived in an apartment and the landlord failed to make certain repairs after a problem had been brought to his attention, would you insist on it?

____ 44. Do you find it difficult to ask your boss or supervisor to let you off early?

____ 45. Do you have difficult verbally expressing love and affection to your spouse, boyfriend, girlfriend?

____ 46. Do you readily express your opinions to others?

____ 47. If a friend makes what you consider to be an unreasonable request, are you able to refuse?

Scoring

The first step in scoring is to reverse score (4 = 0, 3 = 1, 2 = 2, 1 = 3 and 0 = 4) the following items: 7, 8, 9, 10, 11, 12, 13, 15, 16, 18, 19, 21, 24, 27, 28, 31, 34, 35, 42, 43, 44, 46 and 47. Then simply add together your responses to all of the items. Higher scores indicate higher levels of assertiveness.

How did you score? A score of 119 for men and 115 for women is positioned at the 50th percentile for each respectively, so this would be the 'average' score. By definition, all of us fall on a continuum with regard to assertiveness, and we often find that where we stand depends to a large extent on circumstances. That is, for example, we might be generally more assertive at work and less so at home. We may take a leading role in a club and be more laid back when hanging out or deciding what to do with friends. One of the drawbacks of personality tests is that they frequently try to account for a multiplicity of roles. Indeed, many tests such as the one above actually seek to explore a quality across situations for therapeutic reasons. Additionally, it should be noted that the test above was validated by use on college students, and so may not apply as well to other populations (Gay et al., 1975). Still, a test such as this is a good launching point for some consideration and discussion on the quality explored, in this case one's ability to be assertive.

According to its creators, those who scored higher on this test had a tendency to 'more often seek leadership roles in groups' (ibid.: 343). Sometimes we may note that it is a fine line between assertiveness and aggressiveness. Generally speaking, library managers, especially those new to the role, have a tendency not to be very assertive, let alone aggressive, and to lack confidence in demonstrating this behavior. While a good manager generally trusts employees, the reality of the workplace is that conflict does occur. It is most critical on these occasions, for example, that one demonstrate the ability to be assertive. If this is not one's natural tendency then, in an ideal circumstance (i.e. if the conflict does not require your instant attention), the manager should stop to think about what the problem is and how to approach it. One should anticipate objections and emotional responses from others when dealing with the conflict or problem, and have a plan for handling them. Conversely, for those library managers who are perhaps on the other end of the assertiveness spectrum and tend to jump into the fray quickly, the idea of stopping to think things through is equally applicable. In this case, however, someone who knows himself or herself to be very assertive should proceed with caution, and consider if the conflict needs to be met head on or if it can be addressed by simply facilitating discussion between the parties. Again, it comes down to knowing yourself and then applying that knowledge to the task at hand. Is assertiveness required? If so, what is required of me? Do I need to be firm and direct or am I better off simply facilitating? Am I making the decision to approach the problem or issue by leaning towards my tendency to be more or less assertive? What is the outcome that I am looking for?

Another example of a relevant quality worth exploring is empathy. This has been variously described by stating that 'an empathic person can imaginatively take the role of another and can understand and accurately predict that person's thoughts, feelings, and actions' and that it is 'a vicarious emotional response to the perceived emotional experiences of others' (Mehrabian and Epstein, 1972: 525). Among librarians, one tends to find empathy in abundance, especially when it comes to library users and their information needs. That said, a strong degree of empathy is not universal and, in its extreme manifestations, comes with some of its own pitfalls. Like the quality of assertiveness, one can differ considerably on the level of empathy depending on the circumstances. In order to manage employees, however, we must be able to understand them in terms of their needs and concerns. On its most basic level, an employee dealing with a serious problem at home, such as a sick child or parent, is typically not going to function as well without some extra consideration on the part of the manager. This is by no means to say that the manager should make excuses for work not being completed. It is to say that a manager who cannot understand and appropriately address an employee's concerns is going to be less effective. On the other side of the coin is the manager who perhaps empathizes too much with employees and then runs into the opposite problem of, as stated, making excuses and allowing the mission of the library to suffer. If you can determine where you fall in this spectrum, you can begin to ask yourself some important questions when faced with issues. Is there something that is affecting this employee that in turn is affecting their work? Is there something affecting the staff as a whole that needs to be addressed? What kinds of things could I do or accommodations could I make that do not hinder the library's mission to meet the need of an individual employee? If I am a person who tends to be very empathetic, is my accommodation or solution fair to others on the staff or am I setting myself up for problems down the road?

A couple of additional points on empathy will help drive home its importance. One may lean towards the stronger end of the scale when it comes to empathy. Thus, when making a decision, managers need to be aware of this tendency. Failure to do so would lead them to make exceptions for one employee that might not be fair to other employees. This is not to say that all employees are to be treated equally. In fact, authors Marcus Buckingham and Curt Coffman (1999), in their book *First Break All the Rules: What the World's Greatest Managers Do Differently*, make some excellent points in this regard. Someone who is a star in one area may get some extra consideration in another that might not be accorded to a different employee. Still, one needs not just to empathize but to recognize the consequences of making the consideration and also look at the bigger picture, such as the employee's overall contributions and the contributions of other team members. For another example of how empathy moves beyond just the management piece itself and extends to library customers, one could also discuss the role played by student employees. While librarians typically have a passion for assisting, many student employees or younger workers employed in the library come to it as the first job they have ever held. As such, they need to be instructed that students or youth coming in as patrons should not ever be sent away without providing assistance (even if this means getting a librarian to answer a given question). One way to drive the desire for them to have empathy in this regard is to remind them that they too are students or patrons at times, and have them ask themselves how they'd like to be treated if they were on the other side of the desk.

Annual performance reviews/appraisals

Almost every organization conducts annual performance reviews or appraisals, and libraries are no different. These can be a fantastic source for getting to know oneself better and also a chance for one to target areas of growth. Most appraisals consist of elements whereby a manager makes judgments about an employee's performance and the employee self-assesses their performance as well. For example, while the process has varied considerably over time, in recent years Johnson & Wales University in Charlotte has a standardized instrument to be used across campus. This instrument allows a supervisor to rate employees on a scale of 1 to 5 on their written communication, verbal communication, problem-solving abilities, planning activities, motivational ability (if they are a manager), leadership (again, if in a managing role) and administrative abilities. This section will focus on what the university has identified as core competencies. Core competencies tend to be skills that, while identified as specifically relevant by a given institution, are readily transferrable. In terms of its relevance to libraries, a study by Donna Chan found evidence that many medium- and large-sized public libraries in Canada are moving to adopt core competencies in their appraisal process. Examples of such competencies include 'communication skills; interpersonal skills; customer service; analytical skills; accountability; adaptability; technological competence; planning and organizing skills; knowledge of the organization; creativity/innovation; and, leadership' (Chan, 2006: 148). The instrument used at Johnson & Wales also assesses the employee based on specific goals (usually worked out between the manager and employee), and includes a self-assessment with questions such as 'What is your most significant contribution to the organization this past year?'

One of the most difficult issues with annual reviews is that they are often surrounded by a fair amount of stress. If the discussion focused on performance management is connected to a discussion of a raise, then the review process begins to feel like an all-or-nothing proposition whereby the employee is focused almost entirely on what the bottom line is on that latter account. In the words of one author, when connected to pay, 'from an employee perspective, the discussion can become rife with stress and emotion' (Berard, 2004: 28). The employee will not really listen to any other information or process it as deeply. Thus, in many cases, as a manager it is a good idea to differentiate the review/raise processes as much as practical. An effective way to separate the two further is to have more frequent reviews, even if this amounts to just adding a mid-year review. There will typically be no expectations regarding salary on the employees' part in the middle of the year, so they may be more willing to listen and converse. Of course, to get the most out of *your* review and appraisal, you must also try your best to tune out that voice inside your head that is concerned about a raise when being reviewed if the two pieces are connected.

Stress in the review process does not just come from the salary implications. It also comes from the very idea of being judged. No matter what the relationship with a supervisor, this process is loaded with potential pitfalls. Sometimes the relationship between employee and manager is a good one. This has two significant dangers. First, due to the amicable nature of the relationship, the one conducting the review may have a tendency to gloss over any significant problems or mistakes a person has made. This is not helpful for anyone. As an employee, one should encourage the supervisor to share specific and constructive feedback and, likewise, as a library manager, one should be willing to provide it. The flip side is when an employee does not have a good working relationship with a manager. The danger from this perspective is that the employee will simply tune out because of the poor quality of the pre-existing relationship. Again, it is very hard to set aside ego on these occasions and it is very easy to become defensive. That said, regardless of the situation there is usually some truth in what is said. Granted, by 'truth' many times we may be referring to perception, but, as will be discussed with 360-degree feedback, perception is very relevant. How others see us is important, especially if we are in a managerial role. One should take what is said and allow it to sink in for a while. We are usually more apt to accept negative feedback constructively once our emotions have had a chance to settle down and our body no longer feels as though it is in a fight-or-flight situation.

360-degree feedback

Multi-source assessment is another approach that people can take in learning about themselves. Despite the fact that this approach usually requires a level of institutional support, since some organization and planning are needed to administer it, it is worth discussing here. While appraisals delivered by supervisors are of value, they do have the potential of suffering from a number of drawbacks as mentioned above. Additionally, according to Mark Edwards and Ann Ewen (1996: 6–7):

> They may reflect self-serving and other individual biases. Politics, favoritism, and friendship may enter into the assessment. The supervisor may have had an insufficient opportunity or motivation to observe employee performance. The supervisor may be unwilling to confront poor performance. Different supervisors may have degrees of rigor in making evaluation decisions.

It is for these reasons that an organization or individual might turn to a multi-source assessment such as 360-degree feedback. According to Edwards and Ewen, the first published professional literature on this approach dates from 1993. The idea behind 360-degree feedback is to have not just a supervisor but others such as peers, direct subordinates and, in some cases, customers or vendors rate an employee's performance. An example of items rated on a ten-point Likert scale, for example, would be 'supports team goals', 'builds and maintains productive working relationships', 'organizes work', etc. (ibid.: 84–5). The evaluator would select a higher number if the statement relates well to their perception of an employee and a lower number if it does not. The survey is typically administered or at least tabulated electronically.

A couple of common misconceptions exist about 360-degree feedback when employed throughout an organization. One is that it can be done informally without much thought to questions/statements and how it is organized. In contrast, it requires very careful thought in its application. A more common misconception is just the opposite: that there is only one way to conduct such an exercise. Rather, the best way is to utilize a combination of experienced professionals (perhaps outside the organization) and an internal team to come up with questions and an approach that works for a given organization. Ideally, questions should be tailored to relate to the institutional mission and goals.

While not by any means free, the cost of the process is not prohibitive for most large libraries. Even a smaller library that is part of a larger institution may have access to this type of tool. In a small academic library scenario, the library director might be rated by his/her supervisor, direct subordinates and other campus department heads. According to its creators, 'The 360 degree feedback process yields specific and quantitative information for each employee to use in making intelligent career decisions. When work associates are assured that they will remain anonymous, they are willing to provide insight they might not reveal in a face-to-face meeting' (ibid.: 16). In this case, the library director will be able to ascertain how s/he is perceived both as a whole and on a variety of levels within the organization. This can be a powerful tool for understanding oneself. It should come with a few words of caution, however. This tool should really be used for growth purposes, and not appraisal for the sake of raises, etc. While some might disagree with this, because it is such a powerful tool and can be very personal, employees should ideally be given an opportunity to opt in or out of the process when applied across an institution.

Informal feedback and coaching

Another great source of information about oneself is through informal relationships and coaching. Mentors are great. If you are lucky enough to have others you can turn to whom you respect, then you should readily do so. Sometimes this could be a more senior library administrator outside your normal reporting line, and other times it could be a library administrator or other relevant individual not even in the same workplace. In my current situation, for example, I find that my initial response to some problems, affected as it may be by my own subjective perspective, can be tempered considerably by a discussion with our campus's associate dean. In working through problems or dilemmas with a trusted peer, one can learn more about oneself and one's tendencies, and improve some of one's decision-making as a result. The best kind of person is one who can metaphorically 'hold up a mirror' to you so that you can see yourself and your own thought process. It should almost go without saying that this should be someone you trust. One adaptation which has been suggested on this theme, which doesn't work quite as well but does have benefits, is to try and view your actions and behavior as much as possible from a third-party perspective. That is, write down how you behaved or made a decision in a certain situation, and then try to look at both the positives and negatives you would attribute to someone else if the story, incident, etc. was not about you.

Formal coaching is yet another possibility. In the business world there is often money available for corporate coaches who can work with an executive as an objective third-party voice in career planning, problem-solving, etc. Unfortunately, this is not usually an option for a library manager. Still, there are a number of programs out there, such as the Historically Black Colleges and Universities (HBCU) Library Alliance

Leadership program and the ACRL/Harvard Leadership Institute. In relation to the HBCU Library Alliance, a recently appointed colleague of mine, the director of library services at Johnson C. Smith University, Nooma Monika Rhue, states: 'This was an invaluable experience and the networking opportunity is irreplaceable. I left feeling confident that I could call on anyone of my colleagues in the program to help me as a new Library Director. I am sincerely thankful for being a part of the HBCU Leadership Institute' (personal communication, 27 July 2009). I should note that a word of warning is pertinent on the latter program: the ACRL/Harvard Leadership Institute, while truly exceptional in scope and effectiveness, is not typically geared towards new but rather somewhat experienced managers. Before becoming a library manager there are numerous other mentorship programs sponsored by various library associations that you might take advantage of as well. I also highly recommend involvement in the Library Leadership and Management Association (LLAMA) as well, since its mission is to be the premier organization in helping to develop library administrators. In recent years it has placed a much greater emphasis upon recruiting librarians new to management, or even those with just a burgeoning interest in management and leadership.

Daniel Goleman and emotional intelligence

In recent years, Daniel Goleman's theories on emotional intelligence have been applied in a wide variety of situations, from school to work to life in general. According to Goleman (1997: 5), we are hardwired such that 'while our emotions have been wise guides in the evolutionary long run, the new realities civilization presents have arisen with such rapidity that the slow march of evolution cannot keep up'. Essentially, studies of the brain have revealed that the amygdala plays a key role in causing our bodies to respond very rapidly to specific stimuli. The neocortex, that part of our brains which controls higher-order functions and is essentially where our reasoning comes from, is on the other hand much slower to respond. In a nutshell, Goleman posits that as children we learn specific emotional skills which relate to how we deal with this biological fact of life, and that these skills are every bit as critical if not more so than traditionally considered 'intelligence'. Furthermore, while we have certain ingrained tendencies, there are things we can do as adults to improve our skills.

In Goleman's words, emotional intelligence amounts to 'being able to motivate oneself and persist in the face of frustrations; to control impulse and delay gratification; to regulate one's moods and keep distress from swamping our ability to think; to empathize and to hope' (ibid.: 34). Aside from once again highlighting the need for empathy, this list includes a number of critical features for displaying a high level of emotional intelligence. Research has shown that the ability to handle failure and setbacks with some optimism is a significant indicator of future success. More specifically, 'reframing a situation more positively' has been shown to put anger and other negative emotions aside, such that one is able to think more clearly (ibid.: 60). Those who are able to delay gratification tend to be more successful as well. Amazingly, studies of children and their willingness to put off a short-term award in favor of a larger, long-term award showed that this ability translated to greater success in life. Just how important might these abilities related to emotional intelligence be? Studies have shown that 'at best, IQ contributes about 20% to the factors that lead to life success' (ibid.: 34). So it turns out that for all our emphasis on book learning, it is the emotional and social skills learned at home and in school that may actually have the greater value.

In a later book which helped translate his thoughts more directly to management, Goleman, along with Richard Boyatzis and Annie McKee, points out the critical areas for any manager to be aware of. Personal competence includes items such as self-awareness and self-management. These are further broken down to include items such as understanding one's strengths and weaknesses, being more aware of one's emotions and keeping them in check, having confidence in oneself, being able to adapt and achieve, and showing initiative and optimism. Social competence is also important, as it relates to the subcategories of social awareness and relationship management. These are further broken down to include being empathetic in regard to others in the organization, understanding the culture of the organization, providing influence and leadership, having a concern for helping others develop their careers, being able to foster change and handle conflict, and being good at working in a team (Goleman et al., 2002).

All of this is very definitely connected to management in a library situation. Again, we started this chapter with the idea that knowing oneself is important. Goleman might say it is *all*-important. That is, EI as applied to management starts with self-awareness and an ability to exercise control over ourselves and handle social situations in a constructive manner. Librarians and library managers are by no means immune to emotions such as frustration, anger, fear, etc. that can cloud their judgment. One of the most important lessons that Goleman has to teach is the need to keep oneself in check. The ability to become more self-aware and to reframe a situation is critical for a manager. To some extent, this lesson boils down to not just knowing yourself in general but knowing yourself on a given day. Everyone has a bad day. You didn't get much sleep the night before, you found out that your spouse bounced a check, you just had a disagreement with your boss and then, all of a sudden, a patron or library staff member is standing in front of you with a problem. How do you react? Now think about the same staff member or patron standing in front of you after you slept well, had your first cup of Dunkin Donuts coffee and your boss had just called to say you were doing a great job. Do you respond differently? We hope and strive for the response to be thoughtful, concerned and caring in both circumstances, but this may not always be the case. Be aware of your emotions, and don't let them control your next move.

Beyond this general discussion on personal competence, the concept of social competence is very relevant in the library manager's role as well. The ability to build and grow relationships is crucial not just for one's personal growth and success – it is a necessity for the area or library that one manages. Aside from the more obvious importance of the quality of the internal social environment, outsiders will often view certain aspects of the library based on their perception of individuals in leadership positions. These outsiders, whether they are other department heads, patrons, teachers, administrators, community, etc., all have a relationship to the library, and the library manager has a responsibility here. One thing that a library manager has to be concerned about is how s/he represents the library or institution. Being at home and 'out of role' is very different to when one is 'in role' as a library manager. You then need to be acutely conscious of the fact that, at least in some sense, you are the library. If you are not a social bug, you need at least to do your best to get out on occasion and get to know on an individual basis some of the people who represent important library constituencies.

Before leaving the topic of emotional intelligence, it is relevant briefly to share the results of a recent study by Peter Hernon and Nancy Rossiter which involved surveys of job advertisements for library director positions and current library directors (the responses of 70 library directors were included). In the category of self-awareness the most important characteristic was 'cognitive ability to deal with complex scenarios/situations'. Under self-regulation the most important characteristic was 'stable temperament and an ability to maintain an emotional balance under constant tension'. Under motivation the most frequently mentioned trait was 'visionary – able to build a shared vision and rally others around it'. Under empathy, the most often selected choice was 'treat people with dignity/respect', with a close tie for second between 'attract, build, and retain talent' and 'good interpersonal/people skills'. Lastly, under social skills the most often picked choice was 'ability to function in a political environment' (Hernon and Rossiter, 2006: 263–7).

Robert Greenleaf and servant leadership

Again we come to the work of Robert Greenleaf, this time to explore his concepts in relation to how we can better know and grow ourselves. In the discussion above on 360-degree feedback, one might note that knowing how a library manager's direct subordinates see her/him is of considerable value to that individual. In the context of 360-degree feedback it is only one of several perspectives, however, as the perspectives of peers, supervisors and customers are often included as well. In that sense, one might infer that Greenleaf's approach, which focuses exclusively on direct subordinates, is somewhat diminished. To do so would be a mistake. Greenleaf and his philosophies offer some insights that in many ways are deeper and more profound than those that may be attained through 360-degree feedback, as well as other approaches such as traditional performance appraisal.

Like Goleman and Covey (whose ideas are discussed below), Greenleaf puts significant emphasis on self-reflection. He emphasizes the need to 'simply practice being aware', and states that 'to do anything reflectively demands that one be alone with one's thoughts and accept the presence of the deeper self with which one may have only tenuous communication' (Greenleaf, 1996: 36, 43). His emphasis is placed to an extent on the need to meditate and what he refers to as entheos or enthusiasm. To Greenleaf, this quality (i.e. enthusiasm) is much more significant than we normally think. He discusses the need to have the inner strength to make decisions in the face of adversity (realizing these decisions could end in mistakes) and an ability to stay focused even when external incentives would serve to drive us in the wrong direction, to avoid busyness for its own sake and, above all, to be trusting and caring about others. Greenleaf quotes Rousseau in saying that 'we do not lose our way through what we do not know but through what we falsely think we know' (ibid.: 59). For Greenleaf, one way to avoid losing our way is, as mentioned above, through both internal reflection and by listening to and in some sense being grounded by one's staff.

The work of Greenleaf was operationalized on a limited basis by, among others, James Hunter (2006) through his CD training course *Servant Leadership Training Course: Achieving Success through Character, Bravery, and Influence*. This course seeks to provide practical advice on servant leadership. Perhaps its most useful component is an assessment which comes with the CDs. The assessment can be done anonymously by one's staff and then compiled to give managers a better understanding of their own strengths and weaknesses as viewed by staff. For example, the survey may indicate a weakness in focused listening. Further investigation might lead to a discovery that this concern grew out of the manager's constant need to multitask. The library manager might then decide to work on his or her listening skills, or perhaps encourage staff to schedule more focused one-on-one meetings whereby they would promise to drop whatever else they are doing for a short period of time to focus their attention on relevant concerns.

Stephen Covey and the seven habits

Much like Robert Greenleaf's, the work and writings of Stephen Covey are applicable to a variety of topics explored in this book. Covey's work, however, bears special relevance to the topic at hand of knowing oneself. It is also an appropriate way for us to conclude this chapter, since his concepts can be readily applied and can serve as a guide for future development.

He has published numerous other writings and done countless seminars on his ideas, but *Seven Habits of Highly Effective People: Restoring the Character Ethic* is Covey's seminal work. While his book is very clear and easy to understand, I had the good fortune to attend a three-day workshop about ten years ago on his seven habits, and walked away with numerous insights that I am still trying to digest to this day. One of the central tenets of Covey is that too much literature focuses on what he refers to as the 'personality ethic' as opposed to the 'character ethic'. The former is described as a more superficial approach to learning and growth. Writings in this area focus more on 'tricks' or quick fixes, as opposed to focusing on a deeper understanding of oneself. According to Covey (1989: 21–2):

> to focus on technique is like cramming your way through school… In most one shot or short-lived human interactions, you can use the Personality Ethic to get by and to make favorable impressions through charm and skill and pretending to be interested in other people's hobbies. You can pick up quick, easy techniques that may work in short-term situations. But secondary traits alone have no permanent worth in long-term relationships.

Long before it was popular to use the words 'paradigm shift' to indicate a major change in a way of thinking, Covey had applied it to his ideas. His character ethic, in contrast to the personality ethic, focuses on principles. 'Principles are guidelines for human conduct that are proven to have enduring, permanent value.' According to Covey, these values include 'fairness… integrity… honesty… human dignity… service… excellence… potential… growth… patience, nurturance, and encouragement' (ibid.: 34–5). Another related foundational concept of Covey's is maintaining a balance by both actually producing and maintaining one's productive capability, something he calls the P/PC balance. His seven habits are all extremely relevant to any library manager, so it is of value here to address each in turn.

The first habit is to be proactive. Central to being proactive, Covey notes that between each and every stimulus and response there is a moment of choice. We can choose not to be immediately reactive. In Covey's words, 'The ability to subordinate an impulse to a value is the essence of a proactive person' (ibid.: 72). This relates very much, as do other habits, to Goleman's concept of emotional intelligence. As a library manager, one will be pulled in many directions. It is very easy simply to react to that which is around us, as opposed to following our own initiative. Studies have shown that it is common in the realm of communication alone for a library director to be inundated by e-mail on a daily basis, for instance (Hernon et al., 2004). On a micro scale, one might consider how, even in the collection development role, this applies. Librarians are often inundated with catalogs and various vendors' publishing slips or updates. Reliance upon these could cause one to become extremely reactive in developing the collection. That is, as opposed to thinking through issues of balance, one would tend simply to make purchases and additions according to current publishing trends. However, if one forced oneself to be more proactive by actively engaging faculty, examining assigned textbooks for the courses in this area, etc., over time collections would begin to demonstrate greater balance overall. And one last piece of advice attached to this habit is worth mentioning. Managers should focus on their 'circle of influence' and not their 'circle of concern'. That is, Covey reminds us all to spend time focused on the things we can control and not worry about the things that we cannot.

The second habit is to 'begin with the end in mind'. According to Covey (1989: 97–8), 'We may be very busy, we may be very efficient, but we will also be truly effective only when we begin with the end in mind.' One way to focus on this habit is to consider what you would want said about you at your funeral; another way is to write a personal mission statement. Surely every library needs a mission statement to help guide priorities, policies and decision-making. This could be applied at the individual level as well. By thinking about your funeral, or perhaps less morbidly your legacy in the workplace, you might be more inclined to think longer term and make wiser decisions as a result.

Habit three, put first things first, is one of my favorites. Its connection to being proactive and beginning with the end in mind should be obvious. Still, it seems that many people don't put first things first. What can this mean in a library situation? All libraries are pulled in a variety of directions. Academic libraries are not immune. In addition to its traditional role as a warehouse of books, the library's teaching mission has become more and more important in recent years. The academic library is now also often expected to have 'fun books and videos' and a coffee/snack bar, to provide workshops on various topics, sponsor book clubs, etc. The library manager needs to recognize that putting first things first usually means providing reference and instruction services, and then worrying about other concerns and services afterwards. There will be time for the other things, but the focus should first be on one's 'bread and butter'. Priorities must be set both personally and for the library.

Habit four is to think about scenarios that seem oppositional and then try to create a win/win situation. According to Covey (ibid.: 207), 'It's not your way or my way; it's a better way, a higher way.' This is probably the most difficult habit to develop, especially in a world of limited resources. Its dimensions involve 'character... relationships... agreements... structure... systems [and] process' (ibid.: 216). Essentially, we need to be mature in our understanding not just of our needs but those of other parties. We need to recognize that building relationships with others is fundamentally more important than immediate concerns, that agreements need to acknowledge the interdependency of the parties and that systems and processes have to be in place that make good sense for carrying out agreements. Again, library managers face the need to work across departments within and outside the library on a daily basis. Win/win scenarios lead to long-term benefits for the library.

Covey (ibid.: 237) states, 'If I were to summarize in one sentence the single most important principle I have learned in the field of interpersonal relations, it would be this: Seek first to understand, then to be understood.' Through this fifth habit, he ties together two key elements: empathy and listening skills. While the critical importance of empathy to a library manager has been addressed above and the importance of active listening will be discussed in detail in the chapter on communication, it is worth noting how this all fits here. Covey's emphasis in habit five is on empathetic listening. So as we continue to think about understanding ourselves, we need to remember how important the people around us are.

Habit six, while relating to all of the other habits, probably fits best with the win/win concept. In habit six, Covey tells us that we should focus on synergies. That is, we should consider how the sum of the parts is actually greater than the individual parts on their own. Any experienced teacher can relate to this. When a class or groups within a class are truly engaged in meaningful discussion and learning, the ideas of one student feed off another. So too with library staff.

Lastly, a favorite of all fans of education is 'sharpen the saw'. By this, Covey means to place emphasis on our need to continue our growth. It is not enough to know who we are at this moment; rather, we should also be trying to better ourselves on a regular basis. Certainly, management skills are a part of this. In Covey's mind, however, the concept is much grander and includes the 'physical, spiritual, mental, and social/emotional' (ibid.: 289). Indeed, we need to take care of our physical being with exercise, proper diet, etc. We also need the time to think and reflect on a deeper level than when encumbered by distractions of all kinds. We need to engage our minds and explore new ideas. I personally enjoy reading in a wide variety of areas – history, fiction, science, management, education, etc. Additionally, we need to be concerned about our relationships with those important people around us. All of these require us to set very clear priorities and pay close attention to our productivity not just now but in the future as well.

Thoughts for consideration or discussion

- How did you score on the assertiveness scale? How might this illustrate potential strengths and/or challenges you might have as a library manager?

- What kinds of performance appraisal systems are in your local public, academic or school library? If you can chat with someone in the organization, how do they feel about the appraisal system?

- Have you ever been reviewed in a library or other type of job? What were the positive and negative aspects of your experience? What did you learn about yourself?

- What makes a good mentor?

- How do you think others perceive you? Do you think people who see you in the different roles you occupy would say different things about you?

- In considering the idea of emotional intelligence, do you have any strengths that seem to stand out? How about weaknesses?

- Taking the various aspects of emotional intelligence piece by piece, how can you improve your skills, especially as they would relate to managing others?

- How does servant leadership focus more attention back on the leader or manager? Does this concept appeal to you as an approach to leadership and management? Why or why not?

- Of Stephen Covey's 'seven habits', which ones stand out as being most important to you for a manager, and why?

Case study: Jekyll and Hyde?

John had been a library director for 11 months. Prior to this position he had worked for five years as a systems librarian at a large public library and for two years as an emerging technologies librarian at a different public library. The library board of Small Town Public Library (STPL), with its interest in modernizing library services, decided to hire John as the new director. He had no prior managerial experience.

While chatting over lunch, Susie, a senior librarian at STPL, remarked to another librarian, Michael, that John was not working out very well.

He seemed to spend all of his time on the computer, except when he came around to lash out about something with little tact or sensitivity. He also seemed to have no understanding of some basic aspects of the library's operations (such as when it came to programs targeted at the local schoolchildren) and he never seemed to recognize any of the extra work done by others. Michael agreed with the lashing out part, but defended John by saying that at least it only happened on rare occasions when he was 'stressed out'. He also agreed, however, that John knew an awful lot about technology but had made little effort to understand other aspects of library operations. Additionally, he couldn't remember John giving a compliment to anyone. Michael added that he felt he needed more direction from John at times but was afraid to set him off, so he just avoided asking him questions or approaching him for advice except when he really had to.

Meanwhile, at the very same time, Joanne, the chair of the board of directors for STPL, was meeting with the mayor over lunch. Joanne was happy to share with the mayor that the new director had overseen a major change in library services with a much greater emphasis on technology (new computers and layout that encouraged their use, new databases added on, technology classes, etc.). Library usage, in fact, had increased by approximately 50 percent since he took over by gate and circulation count. The mayor couldn't help but get excited and remark upon how good a choice they had made in selecting John.

- What are the issues here with John? How does he appear to be failing or succeeding?

- Just because these two staff members feel this way about John, does it make it true?

- What steps could John take to find out for himself how he is perceived? Can staff have any part in suggesting he needs to do so?

- If, in fact, Susie and Mark's views are congruent with how other staff see him, what can John do about it, assuming that he really does want to be a good manager?

- What about the changes in library usage which appear to be due to John's change in emphasis on services and obvious technology-related skills? How do we square the perception that the chair and now the mayor have of John with the staff perception? How often are managers viewed very differently by different groups (e.g. staff, supervisor, peers, etc.)?

Project ideas

- Research mentoring programs such as that of the ACRL/Harvard Leadership Institute. What do they have to offer? Is it possible to attend or participate in one of these?

- Write a personal mission statement.

- Begin a dialogue with a teacher, mentor or someone who you trust. What areas do you seem to be strong in? What areas might you consider working on and how?

- Review and update your resume. Couple this activity with creating a professional growth plan that identifies specific targets for accomplishing your goals.

3

Motivating employees and fostering diversity

While we will explore it here in greater isolation, the topic of motivation is really not disconnected from the topics already discussed. Any decent general theory of management must consider the critical element of how to motivate employees. Furthermore, understanding motivation also helps to build on the concept of knowing oneself better, as discussed in the previous chapter. It should be noted that anything short of a book is bound just to scratch the surface of the topic of motivation. As such, presented below are some of the better known and most often considered theories and ideas related to the concept.

While fostering diversity may seem an odd fit for a chapter on motivation, it is included because of my personal conviction that diversity in the workplace with regard to work teams can be a great source of motivation. Again, this topic is fairly large, and so relevant highlights are explored. While diversity is considered from traditionally understood perspectives, it is also addressed as a much broader concept, to include consideration of diversity at the individual level as opposed to simply membership in a recognized group.

Needs theories

Virtually all discussions on motivation begin with what are commonly referred to as needs theories. The two seminal figures in this regard are Abraham Maslow and David McClelland. Since Maslow's work is more fundamental, it will be addressed first.

Maslow's theory of motivation focuses on a hierarchy of needs. According to Maslow ([1954] 1987: 56), 'The basic needs arrange themselves in a fairly definite hierarchy on the basis of the principle of relative potency.' The most basic desires of all human beings are physiological. According to Maslow (1943: 373), 'Undoubtedly these physiological needs are the most prepotent of all needs.' Included in this category are items such as access to food and air. Indeed, these are very basic. Maslow states: 'It is quite true that man lives by bread alone – when there is no bread. But what happens when there *is* plenty of bread and when his belly is chronically filled?' (ibid.: 375).

According to Maslow's hierarchy, meeting a more basic need essentially leads to the elevation of the next most prepotent need as a motivator. The next set of concerns beyond the physiological revolve around our need for safety. While implications for how safety needs affect us in the workplace will be discussed, Maslow saw the most basic embodiment of this concept in the behavior of children 'in whom these needs are much more simple and obvious' (ibid.: 376).

Beyond physiological and safety concerns, Maslow argued that love and a sense of belonging would be the next most significant motivational factors. That is, humans have a natural, inborn desire and need to feel as though they belong and that people care about them. This need is not just existent in the family and other social structures, but in the workplace as well (ibid.).

Once basic needs are met, we arrive at what Maslow saw as the first of two higher-order motivators, self-esteem and self-actualization. Since self-esteem can be defined in many ways, it is relevant to quote exactly how Maslow perceived this concept in relation to his theory, as he broke the concept down into what he felt were two distinct subcategories: 'These are, first, the desire for strength, for achievement, for adequacy, for confidence in the face of the world, and for independence and freedom. Secondly, we have what we may call the desire for reputation or prestige (defining it as respect for esteem from other people), recognition, attention, importance or appreciation' (ibid.: 381–2).

Lastly, Maslow's theory posits that the highest-order need or motivator is self-actualization. 'A musician must make music, an artist must paint, a poet must write, if he is to be ultimately happy. What a man *can* be, he *must* be. This need we may call self-actualization' (ibid.: 382).

Some caveats need to be stressed regarding the above-stated theory. As presented in many texts, this theory comes across as very simple and straightforward. Maslow, however, was clear in pointing out some challenges with it from the beginning. He stressed the fact that we typically engage in a given behavior due to *many* different motivational factors – individuals differ for a whole variety of reasons and to a whole array of degrees as to how this theory might apply to them (e.g. someone who has experienced a prolonged period of unemployment might not feel as quickly the need to be motivated by self-actualization as someone with differing past circumstances), and the order as established above may not be quite as rigid in all cases as it would seem.

When discussing Taylor in the first chapter, it was pointed out that while his theories may seem at odds with library work, a basic concern for efficiencies in some areas was applicable. Likewise, with Maslow, while physiological needs may not seem to apply quite as readily to everyday library situations, they are applicable. Consider an employee so dedicated as to continue servicing patrons to such a degree as to sometimes cut into or even skip their lunch break. As a result, their performance and attitude could be negatively affected later in the day. This highlights the simple importance, for example, of making sure that staff get breaks and have basic needs met in this regard. The Hawthorne studies, as basic as they were, clearly demonstrated value towards performance in this regard. While dedicated library staff may be willing to 'soldier through', their motivation and performance could suffer as a result.

As mentioned above, safety is another motivator. In the workplace this often relates to job security and, to some extent, benefits. It is very hard for someone to open themselves up and give their all when there is a question over their future with the organization or their access to critical benefits. As a manager, the relative stability of most organizations needs to be conveyed. While layoffs and cutbacks on benefits are frequently beyond the manager's control (often resting with a higher-level administrator in a university or a principal in a school, for example), s/he needs to be able to convey as much as possible any areas of stability that will or will not be affected by given circumstances. As was mentioned earlier and will be alluded to again in this book, many libraries were recently faced with significant cuts in funding. By knowing what the cuts would be and by management working and communicating with staff to plan for adjusting to the cuts, motivational problems related to safety and security issues were hopefully mitigated to an extent in many different libraries. One other facet of safety relates to an issue which will be addressed in great detail in Chapter 6, the need for trust. According to Kouzes and Posner (1995: 177), 'People must feel safe and secure to develop trust. When contributors' thoughts and ideas are shot down or ridiculed, the climate isn't safe...'

The two higher-order functions of self-esteem and self-actualization are probably the most interesting and relevant to librarians. Many librarians have chosen their profession as a calling, and gain much satisfaction in just knowing that they are doing good work. The self-esteem of a library manager's direct subordinates needs to be a significant consideration on the part of the manager. In the previous chapter, reviews and appraisals as well as other feedback mechanisms were discussed. While these often center on opportunities to look for improvement, they also need to be times to make clear when and how, in a specific way, a given employee is contributing to the library. Furthermore, such feedback should not just be done once a year, but on a fairly regular basis as appropriate achievements and successes occur.

As opposed to the other items mentioned, self-actualization is probably the most difficult area for a manager to have an impact upon. Self-actualization by its definition requires that it comes from the individual. Still, there are things that a manager can do to help create an environment where moments of self-actualization may occur. Supporting the projects and development concerns of staff by providing them with time to work on these is one of the most significant ways to accomplish this. Being available as a sounding board or to bounce ideas off is another.

Maslow himself noted that what he had developed was just a theory. Indeed, researchers have found it somewhat difficult to validate his ideas. Still, hardly anyone would argue against the fact that the ideas provide us with some relevant direction in thinking about the concept of motivation.

Before moving on, I'd like to share an aside on how I believe that even an analogous view of Maslow's theory can be creatively useful in other ways relevant to library management. I was once asked to do a presentation on my 'vision for a highly effective academic library'. I chose to use Maslow's hierarchy concept, replacing, for example, the physiological and safety needs with the core needs of having a library facility, collections and staff. I then worked up towards what I saw as the equivalent of self-actualization of the library or library services, a vibrant and effective information literacy program. In my presentation I was able to relate the concepts quite easily to a crowd of deans and faculty, most of whom were already familiar with Maslow's ideas.

Another key figure in the arena of needs theory is David McClelland. As opposed to a hierarchy, McClelland saw needs arising from three primary motivators: a need to achieve, a need to affiliate with others and a need for power. He developed simple tools for exploring what drives individuals based on these broad concepts, and discovered that people were essentially motivated to a greater or lesser degree by each of these factors (McClelland, 1987).

It has commonly been thought that achievement orientation is somehow 'the best' of these motivators, since it focuses on individual accomplishment. According to McClelland and Burnham (1977: 27), 'Any number of books and articles summarize research studies explaining how the achievement motive is necessary for a person to attain success on his own.' In polling my classes using a very simple instrument based on McClelland's theory, I have found that the overwhelming majority of graduate students studying library science tend to have this type of orientation. Admittedly, this polling is based on a handful of questions as opposed to the more vigorous instruments that McClelland suggests using, such as the analysis of stories that participants are required to write or lab-based experiments they would be put through.

To explore further, what exactly does McClelland mean by achievement? Essentially, the achievement-oriented person tends more readily to accept or set high but reasonable goals and persist. Some experiments have gone so far as to demonstrate that subjects with a high achievement orientation actually display different physiological traits, such as less anxiety when faced with a challenge. They have also been shown to be slightly more sensitive to certain stimuli (McClelland, 1987). Despite the lack of rigor in my polls of students, it seems to make sense that graduate students, often needing to have a clear focus in graduate school while balancing other normal challenges of life, would relate to this kind of approach. It may also be true of most librarians reasonably young or new to the profession – that is, those concerned about building their careers.

To this point it would appear that the achievement orientation is all positive. As stated at the outset, many studies have presumed just this. The problem is that achievement orientation has a price. Because of the need to achieve, people with a high degree of this type of orientation are much less likely to take on something *extraordinarily* challenging. That is, for them goals must be set towards tasks that represent a moderate challenge for them to be most effective. Likewise, any tasks that may be too easy or mundane, however necessary, will not be accomplished as well by someone oriented as such. We shall see also in examining the power orientation that a focus on one's own achievements can become a liability when, as a manager, the focus needs to shift towards the achievement of others in the organization.

The second of McClelland's orientations is affiliation. Those oriented along these lines are concerned about their role in a group or, in our case, the library. They are also very much concerned about relationships within the group. Interestingly, McClelland discusses a test in which subjects are asked to read a case which describes a group of librarians; it hints at but does not overtly reveal their relationships with one another. Subjects are then asked to make guesses about which librarians are closer friends with other staff, which may respect each other but not socialize as much, etc. According to multiple administrations of this test, 'those who score high [in affiliation] tend to *learn affiliative associations faster*' (ibid.: 348). People highest in this orientation can achieve at high levels under particular circumstances. For example, as students they have been shown to perform very well 'in a classroom where the instructor was judged to be warm and friendly' (ibid.: 351). They also attend very well to their interpersonal relationships. Perhaps the single greatest drawback to having this orientation, however, is that people higher in affiliative needs tend to avoid criticism and conflict. Indeed, McClelland reports that studies show people high in this orientation tend to make poor managers.

When it comes to picking a clear 'winner' among his three orientations, he is unequivocal. 'The general conclusion of these studies is that the top manager of a company must possess a high need for power, that is, a concern for influencing people... the top manager's need for power ought to be greater than his need for being liked by people' (McClelland and Burnham, 1977: 28). There are two factors, of course, mentioned here; one is power and the other is a desire to be liked. It should be noted that in a study McClelland later discusses which involved examining the orientations of 50 top managers and the overall morale of their employees, 80 per cent of the employees exhibiting high morale had a manager whose power orientation, whether high or low, was *at least* higher than a concern about being liked. In order to understand the power orientation better and put it into perspective, it is worth a comparison to the affiliative orientation. Someone high in affiliation has been shown to 'make so many ad hominem and ad hoc decisions that they almost totally abandon orderly procedures. Their disregard for procedure leaves employees feeling weak, irresponsible, and without a sense of what might happen next, of where they stand in relation to their manager, or even what they ought to be doing' (ibid.: 36). Again, this highlights the strength of one approach by contrasting it with the weakness of another and, at least in some sense, contrasts it with our common-sense feeling that a 'touchy-feely' manager would always be better from the employee perspective. According to McClelland, this does not mean that a manager can't be democratic when it makes sense (in fact, his data show that both high power and democratically perceived approaches were seen in the profiles of the most effective managers). It just means that they are slightly more focused on the needs of the organization and aligning those with the needs of individuals. For instance, the manager's response to a challenge regarding an initiative would not necessarily be to use his/her power overtly, but to understand better the objections raised and then influence those with objections to adopt the manager's perspective.

What, then, does all of this mean to library managers? In many cases the library manager, even if a director or dean, is not the top administrator in a given system, so the power orientation may not be quite as necessary as McClelland suggests. Still, it is very suggestive. An achievement orientation may be very effective as a graduate student or early in a career when one is trying to prove oneself. It may even be very critical in a smaller organization where the manager engages in *typical* library duties such as reference, instruction or cataloging. Yet even if the individual engages in these tasks, *as a manager* this person will not be judged effective by their success but by those around them. Thus there is a need to influence others, provide some overall vision or sense of direction and keep everyone on what might admittedly be a fairly broad path. In even more concrete terms, the library manager must be concerned about the training and development of subordinates. This can be done in a variety of ways, many of which have already been discussed at length. It also means that the manager needs to channel productivity by saying no to certain projects or convincing staff of the value of certain approaches. In thinking again about the manager's affiliative needs, it is necessary that one is careful not to avoid conflict and negative feedback when it is necessary. For a person new to library management, this can be especially stressful. Attempts in this regard need to be well planned and thought through in advance, focusing on very specific concerns or issues.

Before concluding this discussion, it is worth noting that this section has been structured in such a way as to foster specific further consideration of both Maslow's and McClelland's theories. Maslow's theory was discussed primarily from the perspective of motivating employees and McClelland's from the perspective of the manager. Each theory has relevance, however, if alternatively considered. For example, we might not just give consideration to the motivations of employees along the lines of Maslow's theory, but consider our own behaviors as well. In terms of McClelland, we might also consider how the management of people with different orientations might be affected. For example, in our consideration of diversity below, it is important to note the value of having different approaches on a team. Someone high in achievement might be given specific critical responsibilities that require a high level of achievement for success. Someone with a high affiliative bent could be a useful team member in assisting with activities that require a significant degree of coordination among the group. Someone with a high power orientation might be given a wide degree of influence or latitude in a broadly critical area and/or groomed as a future library administrator.

Motivator-hygiene theory

The seminal figure in motivation-hygiene theory is Frederick Herzberg. Herzberg's theory shares many similarities with those of Maslow and McClelland, but also differs fundamentally in its focus. Herzberg, in turn, gives credit to Elton Mayo for providing a foundation for his work. In his discussion of studies of attitudes in relation to motivation, he states: 'One of the most important is to be found in the pioneering work of Elton Mayo and his colleagues at the Harvard Business School' (Herzberg et al., [1959] 1993: 8). At the core of Herzberg's theory, factors that are dissatisfiers and factors that are satisfiers, and thus positive motivators, are fundamentally different from one another. For example, motivational factors that are satisfiers are 'achievement, interesting work, increased responsibility, growth, and advancement'. On the flip side, 'what makes people unhappy at work is not what they do but how well (or poorly) they are treated'. Herzberg (1974b: 18) goes on to state: 'Because these negative factors describe the job context and, in their negative aspects, serve to provide job dissatisfaction, we have called them hygiene factors.'

In order to explain hygiene better, Herzberg essentially describes a number of typical situations which may arise within an organization that can negatively impact on morale and motivation. Before explaining further, I would like to offer an alternative example relevant to the world of library administration and the assessment of library services that provides an analogous explanation of the hygiene concept. All libraries need to assess their services. One tool developed for this purpose is called LibQUAL+. It is an instrument which measures the perceptions of users against both their minimal and their ideal level of adequacy relative to a given area, such as the library as place or, more specifically, whether or not the library provides a comfortable place to study, for example. The designers of the instrument have described what they refer to as a 'cliff effect'. For example, the temperature of the library does not show up as a comment or concern on a survey of a library until, say, the air-conditioning system breaks for a week or perhaps proves inadequate to handle new space additions. Thus the temperature of the library is not a factor until it becomes a major concern. This is somewhat the same case with hygiene factors. When all is well they tend to blend into the background and don't seem to provide any great bonus towards motivation. When they are a problem, however, they can become a big problem.

In order to develop his models, Herzberg essentially, through separate interviews, focused employees' attention on times when they felt very good or very bad about their given organization. In developing his models, he discovered some interesting points which can generally relate to most if not all circumstances. According to Herzberg (ibid.: 19), 'The most common dissatisfier is company policy and administration...' Conversely, the most important motivators relate to issues that are experienced less frequently, such as personal growth. That is, while a person may encounter policy challenges on a daily or weekly basis, they feel a sense of having experienced significant growth only infrequently.

One of Herzberg's models considers an organization in which a single hygiene factor has emerged as a problem. For his example, he uses a salary problem as an issue. Indeed, in my tenure serving on a non-profit board, I experienced this situation directly. At the time, the organization was viewed as being highly successful on all fronts but one, employee turnover. Some of the most highly valued staff were being lost on a regular basis. A subsequent study indicated that pay was exceptionally low relative to other similar organizations. As a result, the board implemented a specific plan to raise salaries over time. While librarians often earn very modest salaries, concerns arising from comparison to other libraries are very relevant. The implications of this will be made even clearer in the discussion below on equity theory.

Another case which Herzberg mentions is a crisis situation relative to one category. For example, a supervisor suddenly appears so out of line in the perceptions of the staff that a change needs to be made immediately. I have seen this occur as well. Immediate action, as Herzberg recommends, was taken, leaving the organization healthier in the long run. One warning which he offers in this case, however, also bears relevance to a discussion of management. The new leader of the organization, once chosen, was quickly and very clearly empowered so as not to encourage staff to think that, by making the change, they would now be allowed to circumvent the authority of the new manager on an ongoing basis by going over her head.

It is worth a brief mention of two other hygiene-oriented cases which Herzberg posits: a satisfying hygiene effect and a hygiene shock. The former involves a situation whereby the alleviation of a hygiene problem is expected to increase performance over the long run. According to Herzberg (ibid.: 24), 'by expecting increased performance and satisfaction with the job as a result of the alleviation of pain, serious and long-term motivational problems will develop'. This, again, goes back to the premise that hygiene factors have a greater impact as negatives and are not long-term motivators. The hygiene shock concept mentioned above is illustrated by a major external threat to the organization. Again we can use the recent economic downturn beginning in 2008 to illustrate. Initial evidence suggests that organizations which dealt with this proactively and quickly, as Herzberg suggests, when faced with a hygiene shock seem to have fared better than those that did not.

On the other side of Herzberg's hygiene-motivation theory, he describes two cases where positive motivators, or lack thereof, are the main issues to be addressed. In one instance he refers to an 'assembly-line syndrome'. He states that 'It's only the severe constraints placed on opportunities for growth among assembly-line workers that make it appear that they are less interested in motivators... the reality of the situation is quite the opposite' (ibid.: 27). Basically, what Herzberg is saying is that in roles that perhaps require less creativity or critical thinking, it is actually *more* important to consider motivational factors. Failure to do so results in a self-fulfilling prophecy. Thus Taylor's comments mentioned in Chapter 1 where he refers to some workers as being 'stupid' could lead to less motivated workers when the comments lead to a theory in use. In Herzberg's view, which would surely be shared by many others, 'Taylorism is no longer efficient and is out as a viable managerial philosophy' (Herzberg, 1974a: 52). Certainly, most of us would agree that from a motivational perspective, it falls woefully short. In a library situation this might serve as a reminder, while being realistic, not to 'dumb down' our expectations and concerns for paraprofessional, volunteer or student staff.

In another typical case mentioned by Herzberg, individuals may not be given responsibilities commensurate with their abilities. This leads to a failure to motivate. This situation can, however, be rectified by what he refers to as job enrichment (ibid.). By enrichment, he refers not to piling on extra work, but finding rich and meaningful outlets for talented staff. According to Herzberg (ibid.: 54), 'orthodox job enrichment is the most promising of all the organizational improvement strategies'. Within this concept Herzberg refers to 'vertical job loading'. He provides a list of seven concrete examples of how this might be applied to motivate an employee:

- removing some controls while retaining accountability
- increasing the accountability of individuals for their own work
- giving a person a complete natural unit (module, division, area and so on)
- granting additional authority to employees in their activity – job freedom
- making periodic reports directly available to the workers themselves rather than to supervisors
- introducing new and more difficult tasks not previously handled
- assigning individuals specific or specialized tasks, enabling them to become experts (Herzberg, 1968: 59).

Clearly, all the above are very relevant to library work and any combination could be applied, especially to employees who have already shown promise in their currently assigned tasks. In his summary of Herzberg's theory applied in a library environment, Olorunsola (2007: 26) states, 'The basic idea of job enrichment is to give employees at all levels more opportunities to make decisions about their goals, schedules, and methods of doing their job.'

Equity theory

Equity theory in some sense is related to motivation-hygiene theory, in that it considers both demotivators and motivators. It does so, however, at the same time. According to J. Stacy Adams (1963: 422):

> Whenever two individuals exchange anything, there is the possibility that one or both of them will feel that the exchange was inequitable. Such is frequently the case when a man exchanges his services for pay. On the man's side of the exchange are his education, intelligence, experience, training, skill, seniority, age,

sex, ethnic background, social status, and very importantly, the effort he expends on the job.

In a nutshell, workers both consciously and unconsciously consider what they bring to the table when they work for an organization. Beyond this, they make comparisons as to how equitably they are treated relative to others. In Adams's terminology, a 'Person' makes an investment. They then consider outcomes such as 'pay, rewards intrinsic to the job, seniority benefits, fringe benefits, job status' and other factors (ibid.: 423). According to Adams, 'Inequity exists for Person whenever his perceived job inputs and/or outcomes stand psychologically in an obverse relation to what he perceives are the inputs and/or outcomes of the Other' (ibid.: 424). It should be noted that what matters is not necessarily actual but perceived inequity. It should also be noted that, while the Other is typically a co-worker, it could be someone doing similar work in another organization or library.

What, then, does this mean? How does this affect motivation and behavior in general? Studies indicate that individuals will experience cognitive dissonance under inequitable circumstances. Thus if a library staff member perceives that s/he is doing more work than another staff member and being paid at the same rate, s/he would have a tendency to seek equity. This might translate into anything from asking for a raise to decreasing work effort. According to Adams, the most common and readily accessible avenue for an employee feeling this way is to reduce the work effort (ibid.; Cosier and Dalton, 1983).

This theory is fairly straightforward, but comes with its own set of complications. Individuals may differ considerably in what they perceive as inequitable treatment. Furthermore, with regard to extreme incidents, Richard Cosier and Dan Dalton (1983: 316) state that it 'has only marginal explanatory power'. Thus when someone goes as far as quitting due to a perceived injustice, this is typically just the 'straw that broke the camel's back'. Therefore, addressing the one specific grievance of an employee at that point may not really address the other issues. It is also complicated by the fact that, as mentioned, an individual may have as a point of reference someone outside as well as inside the organization doing the same or similar work.

There are some things that a library manager may do to address these issues when they arise. On a basic level, one might suggest consideration of whether or not the perception is a reality. In some cases an employee may not be aware of the contributions of another employee. That said, this does not in itself provide a remedy. Still, since equity is not just about pay, other considerations may be made. For example, a librarian who is receiving inequitable treatment might be given additional benefits (e.g. perhaps travel to a conference) or some additional status (i.e. change of job title). Adams (1963) points out that the Catch 22 of this approach is that individuals then sometimes change the person they compare themselves with to someone of higher status and salary, creating a new equity issue in the long run. A special, somewhat related consideration may be added here. It has been suggested that the equity issue may arise suddenly, as mentioned above, but for *outside* reasons such as an unexpected bill of such a size that a person's attention to the pay equity issue becomes prominent. Conversely, however, it must also be noted that people differ, and they do so beyond strict work considerations, in that most people are motivated in a variety of other ways to mitigate this very thing. For example, a librarian may place a greater value on a flexible work schedule in order to spend time with family, as opposed to higher pay. They may also have to work within certain geographical constraints, and need to weigh that in as well.

One last suggestion by Cosier and Dalton (1983) is to provide an appeal process or a way for employees to address equity concerns more directly. They believe that just having an outlet to express concerns might even help to some extent to reduce tensions.

Victor Vroom and expectancy theory

Victor Vroom is well known for his expectancy theory of motivation. It is similar to equity theory in that it posits that one weighs certain factors relative to motivation. According to Vroom ([1964] 1995: 7), motivation may be defined in a variety of ways, but his definition is 'to refer to a process governing choices made by persons or lower organisms among alternative forms of voluntary activity'. Vroom's theory differs from others to some extent, in that it focuses on the here and now as opposed to past behavior. According to Vroom, his approach forces one to 'assume that the choices made by a person among alternative courses of action are lawfully related to psychological events occurring contemporaneously with the behavior' (ibid.: 17).

The concept of valence is central to Vroom's theory. Essentially, whenever people act, they do so to affect one among two or a series of possible outcomes. Valence is thus 'affective orientations toward particular outcomes' (ibid.: 18). It should be noted that much like equity theory, which focuses on perceived inequity, the focus is on one's *perception* of the outcomes. That is, an outcome may or may not be a satisfier to the degree expected once achieved, but the theory considers only the expected satisfaction to be achieved. In all decisions there is an element of risk. According to Vroom, people essentially weigh their desire to achieve a given outcome against the risk associated with it. He believes that all of these factors can be measured with some degree of accuracy.

Vroom validated his theory in a variety of ways. One way was to ask individuals to report verbally on the elements mentioned above. Another was to analyze fantasies or stories told by individuals. A third was to examine whether or not a given outcome spurred desire in the direction of further learning. A fourth way was to examine alternative choices that an individual could have made against the one actually made. Lastly, one could observe another's actions to see which choices are made. All of these methods allow us to examine motivations relative to Vroom's theory.

While this concept may seem fairly complicated on the surface, it could be applied by library managers with considerable effectiveness. By understanding someone's choices as they are made, their tolerance for risk, etc., one can better guide and coach a given employee. Certainly, individuals will differ considerably in the choices they make and their level of tolerance for risk.

Vroom's book *Work and Motivation*, through its detailed exploration of scores of specific studies, provides much wisdom beyond just the basic outlines of his theory. According to Vroom (ibid.: 46), 'many work roles provide their occupants with an opportunity to contribute to the happiness and well-being of their fellow man'. I can think of no better way to describe how many of us, at least to some degree, view library work. Our respective missions provide us with a great deal of satisfaction and, as he posits, may create a situation in which expenditure of energy as opposed to avoidance of it is deeply satisfying. Likewise, he suggests that some professions are more of a first choice than others. In this respect, one would think that librarians are somewhat unusual in that most, while they may be able to point to positive early experiences in a library, come to the profession later in life. By definition, a librarian is typically not viewed as a professional without a graduate degree in library and information studies. This has significant ramifications for how to motivate professional library staff. He also notes studies which indicate that social workers and teachers are much higher in intrinsic and lower in extrinsic orientation towards rewards. This too may apply to librarians to an equal degree.

Common to all workers, Vroom identifies the most critical satisfiers, which may in turn serve as motivators: 'intrinsic job satisfaction, company involvement, financial and job status satisfaction, and pride in group performance' (ibid.: 118). Some other common elements among workers have been identified by Vroom as well. For example, people commonly list co-workers most often and a supervisor second most often when asked about satisfiers. Likewise, a different *ranked* list of job factors was reported: 'security, followed by opportunity for advancement, company and management, wages, intrinsic aspects of jobs, supervision, social aspects of jobs, communication, working conditions, and benefits…' (ibid.: 123). It should be noted, however, that many of these satisfiers may not directly relate to performance. Certainly, motivation-hygiene theory has already sounded this warning. Vroom (ibid.: 218) states 'There is no simple relationship between job satisfaction and job performance.' While part of this may be due to the challenge in objectively measuring job performance, it also serves as a warning beyond meeting serious hygiene concerns. That is, *just* satisfying people or making them happy is not necessarily the best way for a library manager to motivate staff to be productive. Likewise, while some have suggested that certain styles of management are more conducive to motivation, indiscriminate support or rewarding of staff without connection to performance is counterproductive. 'To be of maximal value to motivating subordinates to perform effectively, consideration or supportiveness must be a response to effort and accomplishment rather than indiscriminate supervisory style' (ibid.: 253). In a separate work, Vroom gets more specific on management styles and notes, for example, that 'managers must have the capabilities of being both participative and autocratic and of knowing when to employ each' (Vroom and Jago, 1988: 42).

Edwin Locke and goal-setting theory

Edwin Locke, along with others, has helped popularize goal-setting theory in recent years. According to Locke and Latham (2002: 705):

> Goal-setting theory was formulated inductively largely on the basis of our empirical research conducted over nearly four decades. It is

based on Ryan's (1970) premise that conscious goals affect action. A goal is the object or aim of an action, for example, to attain a specific standard of proficiency, usually within a specified time limit.

Locke and Latham's theory focuses on conscious choices and thus contrasts with McClelland's and other theories that focus on subconscious motivators. They state that, according to their findings, 'the goal-performance relationship is strongest when people are committed to their goals' (ibid.: 707). Again, this seems to highlight the conscious nature of the theory and hints at other important factors as well. The authors also share the importance of having 'proximal goals' for complex tasks (ibid.: 709).

Over their many decades of research, important aspects of goal-setting have been discovered in addition to those mentioned above. Most fundamentally, much like Covey and Goleman, Locke and Latham emphasize the critical importance of self-efficacy. People with higher self-efficacy tend to set higher goals for themselves and are more positive about receiving negative feedback. Furthermore, they discovered that specific and difficult goals led to higher performance, especially among those with high self-efficacy. People with clear goals established also tended to persist to a greater degree and use more effective strategies to reach goals. So the aim of a library manager might then be most fundamentally to address the broader trait of self-efficacy among library employees. Locke and Latham emphasize three critical ways of doing this: provide access to training and professional development, serve as a good role model and show confidence in an employee's capability and/or potential (ibid.).

There is a lot here of value to the library manager. While Locke and Latham provide good advice, the question remains as to how a manager might apply this in practical ways. Aside from their day-to-day behavior, ongoing feedback, supporting employees through training and expressing confidence on a regular basis, annual appraisals could be seen as a particularly useful time to apply this theory and approach. Clearly, as stated, employees must be committed to their goals. If those can be crafted through a dialogue between the employee and library manager, they can meet the twin needs of generating commitment and assuring institutional alignment.

Locke and Somers (1987) illustrate how this theory was creatively applied in a particular circumstance. They highlight the case of a colonel serving as staff judge advocate for Tactical Air Command, a division of the US Air Force that handles courts martial. According to the authors, this particular unit had been suffering from significantly poor performance, specifically by processing fewer cases than expected. Under the leadership of Colonel David Morehouse it was able to improve performance dramatically. Morehouse achieved this by, among other things, sending monthly letters and communicating by telephone on a regular basis with JA offices. His communications focused on a very specific goal-setting approach which included the following: 'Direct requests to meet goals or improve performance... Practical reasons for meeting the goals... Feedback showing performance in relation to goals... Encouragement and expression of confidence and success... Praise and recognition for accomplishments... Suggestions regarding effective task strategies...' (ibid.: 407) There is no reason why all of these could not apply in a library situation, except that one would expect the communication to be more frequently in person.

Other ways to motivate

There are innumerable ways to reward and motivate employees. Aside from following the theories mentioned above, there is something to the saying that it is the little things that count. Verbal praise is great, but one could become more creative with rewards in order to enhance motivation as well. Bob Nelson is well known for his brief workshops and book, *1001 Ways to Reward Employees*. His book (Nelson, 2005) is a treasure trove of the variety of ways that real people are doing specific things in this regard. There are, of course, any number of special recognition programs that serve as motivators which have been created by libraries, most notably public libraries. The Public Library of Charlotte and Mecklenburg County, for example, has two kinds of awards which it gives to employees, one for special positive feedback from other staff and another for special feedback from patrons.

Diversity and respect

As stated at the outset, diversity could fit in many places in this book. It is often treated as an aside, but is really critical to motivation and success. According to David Thomas and Robin Ely (2001: 34), 'A more diverse workforce... will increase organizational effectiveness. It will lift morale...'

Where should we start with diversity? A comprehensive and integrated approach is necessary, but starting with the basics is relevant here as well. According to Parshotam Dass and Barbara Parker (1999: 69), 'Researchers examining how organizations manage workforce diversity have identified three different perspectives: the discrimination and fairness paradigm, the access and legitimacy paradigm, and the learning and effectiveness paradigm.' The first one is very basic indeed. It focuses attention specifically on laws and quotas. It has its place, but is also very limited and not an effective approach on its own. The second approach also has value, but is limiting in different ways. It focuses more upon quick, bottom-line reasons for adopting diversity as a goal. For example, a company might be interested in tapping a local market of Mexican-Americans and thus decide to employ someone from this group. The third paradigm is very different. It has the 'purpose of learning from employees' different perspectives' (ibid.: 72).

Again, there is some value to understanding the basic legalities associated with diversity issues. Management needs to take this very seriously. One author has wisely suggested a zero-tolerance approach in this regard. Issues of discrimination and sexual harassment can occur in any workplace and libraries are definitely not immune. Libraries or the institutions they are a part of must have a written policy regarding harassment and discrimination. They must also live their commitment to it through training for all employees. This training needs to focus on and provide concrete examples of improper behavior. It also needs to be emphasized that anything approaching this kind of behavior will not be tolerated. Michael Verespej (1997: 27) notes that a common mistake is 'not addressing the so-called low-level violations in the workplace – whether it be offensive graffiti or racial or ethnic jokes – as they occur'.

While hiring ethnic minorities to target new markets may be seen from a cynical perspective in the for-profit world, this might be viewed a bit differently in the library world. In the case of libraries, especially public libraries, for example, it is not inappropriate to try to recruit qualified personnel who can connect with the community. I would argue, however, that the emphasis should be on the ability to communicate better with an important group as opposed to targeting a specific ethnicity in the recruited employee (admittedly, this would probably be a by-product of doing so). Thus a library patronized by a Spanish-speaking community placing an emphasis on hiring someone with Spanish-speaking skills is entirely appropriate.

As stated earlier, the last approach or paradigm is the most productive and generally where we are headed. Having a diverse group of employees with a wide array of different experiences can provide many benefits. While their membership in a group may have helped form their perspective through common experiences, their contributions will be as unique individuals. In order to set up an environment where this kind of diversity thrives, Thomas and Ely (1996) suggest having value for a diverse set of opinions, an understanding of the fact that there will be some challenges in managing a less homogeneous group but that the long-term advantages outweigh any short-term disadvantages, an emphasis on high standards for all employees, support for professional development and openness, an approach which clearly recognizes employee contributions, a clear mission and a relatively flat structure with only minimally necessary bureaucracy. To the foremost points, according to research cited by Kouzes and Posner (1995: 162), 'diverse teams close the performance gap with teams of like individuals and begin to take the lead in the range of perspectives they examine and in the generation of multiple alternatives'.

Thoughts for consideration or discussion

- How do you see Maslow's hierarchy of needs affecting motivation in the workplace and in other situations?

- How do you see yourself relative to McClelland's needs theory? If you were to guess, which orientation do you think fits you or can you relate to most?

- In terms of equity theory, have you ever compared your inputs and outcomes against someone else's inputs and outcomes? If so, did this have any effect on your motivation?

- How much risk are you typically willing to take to accomplish something? Does it need to be easily achievable, moderately achievable, or can it even be almost impossible to achieve?

- What kinds of goals do you set for yourself and how do you go about setting them?

- How do you view diversity in the workplace?

Case study: John needs to light a fire

John was recently hired to become head of reference, a newly created position at North State University (NSU). While he was excited about his new role, he was also a bit anxious. There were three other reference librarians. All seemed to care about students and provided at least adequate coverage and assistance when assigned to the reference desk. A secondary part of their job descriptions (which had not previously been consistently applied), however, stated that reference librarians at NSU needed to publish, become engaged in professional associations, assist on university committees and help with instruction as needed. In these latter areas, at least two of them seemed to fall short. Susie, the library director, met with John about taking on his new role. She was very supportive, but drew attention to the problem mentioned above. To Susie, innovation and awareness of issues and changes in the profession and on campus were critical elements missing from the reference staff. It was made clear that his effectiveness would be judged by how big an impact he could have on motivating staff to address their secondary duties.

John first met with Jean. Jean was the newest librarian, hired right out of graduate school two years earlier. Jean seemed very enthusiastic and appeared the most interested in being involved in the profession. At her own expense, she had recently attended an American Library Association annual conference and a state library conference. She had written a short article for the local library association as well, and served on the campus Wellness Committee. At the start of the current academic year she volunteered to assist with instruction efforts, but found it difficult due to her assigned desk times to audit some sessions (a first step recommended by the two instruction librarians). In John's talk with her, Jean expressed her interest in 'doing better' and 'learning more', but also hinted that it was often beyond her financial means to go to conferences and participate in training on a regular basis. She also hinted that she would consider leaving NSU some day for a job that could provide this kind of support.

Next, John met with Larry. Larry had been with NSU as a reference librarian for ten years. Students frequently commented about how helpful Larry was at the desk. Still, he had not served on a university committee for four years, had not been to any conferences in several years and had never published. He did do some instruction, but only for one faculty member with whom he was close friends. His lesson plan for this class had been the same for the past six years. In discussing the matter with him, Larry related to John that he 'just wanted to help the students' and he didn't see why these other activities were necessary. He also didn't see why he needed to do much more instruction and suggested that, since his session was a good one, there was no need to consider any changes.

Lastly, John met with Lucy. Lucy was also a good reference librarian, as judged by her interactions with students, and had been with NSU for 14 years. She did complain a lot, however, about students 'just wanting to use the internet' and 'always insisting on using electronic sources'. Lucy made it clear to John in their discussion that she felt all the best reference sources were still to be found in paper format. Lucy had been on the university's Orientation Planning Committee for the past ten consecutive years, but had not participated in other university committees. She had once attended an American Library Association conference 11 years earlier and had attended the state library conference when it was in town four years earlier. She had done some instruction in the past, but had been so critical of electronic resources that the instruction librarians had asked the director to have her temporarily excused from these duties.

- How does John motivate the staff to take on more responsibility with regard to the secondary aspects of their job descriptions?

- Should John address the group as a whole, individually, or both about his concerns?

- What issues exist with Jean? Could she actually help him, since she seems to be more eager than the others to become engaged?

- What issues may exist with Larry? How might his comments about the students be used to motivate him?

- What issues may exist with Lucy? How might her comments about providing students with access to the best resources be used to motivate her?

- Does John need more support from the director? If so, what kind of help might be provided?

Case study: action needed

Martin had been the library director for Sunnyville Community College (SCC) for several years. He had a good relationship with other department chairs on campus and was friendly with many of them. The atmosphere among library staff was very friendly as well, with most staff going so far as to socialize outside of work on a fairly regular basis. In passing one day, Martin overheard Lucy and John at their desks talking. It sounded as though Lucy was telling John a joke. The only word he could make out for sure was 'priest'. The next day, John e-mailed a joke to both Martin and Lucy that had the title 'You might be a Jew if...' Martin shook his head and, just as he was thinking of how to address what seemed to be becoming a pattern of behavior among staff, another librarian, Melinda, walked into his office and asked to speak with him. She had just been called 'sweetheart' by George, the director of facilities for SCC. She informed Martin that he had also put his hand on her shoulder a couple of times as he was speaking with her in the past. His behavior was beginning to make her feel uncomfortable. She hadn't wanted to say anything earlier because she felt that George was 'basically a nice man' and she didn't want to get him in trouble. Still, she felt that her motivation to come to work and do her job was beginning to suffer as a result of how she felt.

- What are the issues that Martin has to face here?
- What steps does Martin need to take with the staff and other department heads?
- Does it seem like there is a pattern here that could apply to the organization? If so, what can be done about it?

Project ideas

- Read the articles by Robertson (2006) and Nicholson (2003). Now, alone or in a group, consider yourself assigned with the following task for a large public library. You are to come up with a plan or list of ideas to help motivate the following groups: experienced/veteran librarians (those with ten years or more as a professional); younger librarians or those new to the profession; librarians who are already high performing; and/or librarians who are performing poorly.
- Write a list of what you believe your strongest motivators and demotivators are. Share and compare the list with a colleague or classmate.

- Reflect upon and write down on paper a list of experiences in your background that might shape your views on libraries or work in general, and how your background might positively affect your problem-solving abilities. Share these with someone else to explore differences and similarities.

4

Organizational culture and socialization processes

I recently conducted a study of the perceptions of library science students and practicing librarians on the use of case studies in library science education. Of the 34 librarians who responded to the survey, half had eight or more years of experience. This group, consisting as it did of many veteran library staff, several of whom had significant administrative experience as well, indicated that case studies were a valuable learning tool. It is important to note, however, that in their comments they listed some caveats. Perhaps the most significant of these was the need to be able to grasp the organizational culture in order to place a given incident or problem in context. Two comments are particularly illustrative. When asked about the shortcomings of most case studies, two respondents wrote that they 'don't really allow one to understand the organizational culture in which the problem discussed takes place' and 'until you learn the landscape of your own workplace environment, you cannot rely upon what you learned in the classroom to solve most of your problems' (Moniz, 2009). This highlights the critical importance of being able to understand what is meant by organizational culture, how to determine organizational culture, how subcultures differ, how socialization processes work and how to foster change in organizational culture.

Organizational culture: what is it and where did it come from?

The Social Psychology of Organizations by Daniel Katz and Robert Kahn is a classic management text dealing with a number of issues but focusing primarily on organizational culture. According to Katz and Kahn (1966), organizational culture may be viewed to a significant extent through the application of Lewin's open systems theory discussed in Chapter 1. Furthermore, they define organizational culture as follows:

> Every organization develops its own culture or climate, with its own taboos, folkways, and mores. The climate or culture of the system reflects both the norms and values of the formal system. Organizational climate also reflects the history of internal and external struggles, the types of people the organization attracts, its work processes and physical layout, the modes of communication, and the exercise of authority in the system. (Ibid.: 65–6)

In effect, to them the culture question is both very broad and deep. Edgar Schein, probably the foremost expert on organizational culture, in turn focuses especially on the concept of assumptions when defining it. For example, in relation to decision-making, he states, 'A fundamental part of every culture is a set of assumptions about what is real and how one determines what is relevant information, and how to determine whether they have enough of it to decide whether or not to act, and what action to take' (Schein, 2004: 140). Both definitions demonstrate the need to go to the very core of an organization. Schein's emphasis further indicates that reality itself is defined by organizational culture. With regard to stable cultures, he goes so far as to state that 'basic assumptions are so taken for granted that someone who does not hold them is viewed as a "foreigner" or as "crazy" and is automatically dismissed' (ibid.: 25).

It is important to divert here and consider the implications for libraries. Libraries, like all organizations, have a culture. While the library may also have subcultures, as a whole it will typically have shared elements, as noted above. According to Thomas Shaughnessy (1988: 7):

> every library seems to have its own special 'feel' and every staff its own unique value system... In some libraries, it is almost fun to go to work. There is an underlying assumption that jobs are important, employees are valued, and things are happening. Most people want to be part of a winning team, and some organizations (including libraries) are characterized by this spirit. The culture of such organizations lends emotional content to one's work, and helps to personalize the workplace.

Certainly, this paints the picture of a very positive library culture. Of course, the opposite could be true – staff may defect as soon as possible from a highly dysfunctional situation. In practice, most cultures have a mix of positives and negatives that come to be viewed as 'the way we do things'.

This 'way of doing things' essentially springs from three different sources. Schein (2004: 225) notes these as '(1) the beliefs, values, and assumptions of founders of organizations; (2) the learning experiences of group members as their organization evolves; (3) new beliefs, values, and assumptions brought in by new members and leaders.' I may have some unique insight into the process of organizational culture creation implied here. In 2004 Johnson & Wales University opened a new campus in Charlotte, NC. In doing so, it began 'teaching out' programs sponsored at the Norfolk, VA, and Charleston, SC, campuses, as these were to be folded into the new Charlotte campus in the long run. As part of the process, staff and faculty from those campuses were given first choice of positions in Charlotte; the university then opened up the remaining positions to the rest of the Johnson & Wales campuses and the outside in general. As a result, I ended up leaving the North Miami, FL, campus to start the Charlotte campus library. Ultimately, I was one of several Florida staff to move to Charlotte, along with scores of staff and faculty from the Charleston and Norfolk campuses, some employees from the Providence campus and scores of people just plain new to Johnson & Wales. One of the first comments I remember our vice president making to us was that, in effect, we would no longer be a Norfolk, Charleston, North Miami or Providence culture (he had come from the Charleston campus). Rather, we would build our own unique 'Charlotte culture'. So, here we were, working for an institution founded in 1914 in Providence, RI, that had very clear and very stable organizational values (e.g. our emphasis on hands-on learning) and needed to integrate what were, in effect, several different interpretations of those founding values into a new culture. Our earliest days often involved conflict or growing pains in this regard (I was not immune to this; at one point I was asked to avoid starting sentences 'In Florida what we did is...'). One highly rewarding aspect of this process was the opportunity essentially to build a library culture from the ground up. This is not a typical situation – it is much more common to inherit a culture. In this case, it becomes paramount to understand issues associated with changing cultures, which will be discussed further below.

Organizational culture: how do we know what it is in a given organization?

Learning about the culture of an organization can be an exciting but also challenging endeavor. A whole series of items need to be examined, and even then it can remain a relatively elusive picture. This is due to the overall complexity of organizations and the fact that they are constantly changing in small and large ways due to both internal and external pressures. The importance of understanding the culture is critical, however, according to Schein (ibid.: 10), because 'if we understand culture better we will understand ourselves – better understand the forces acting within us that define who we are, that reflect the groups with which we identify and to which we want to belong'. Aside from the implications about subcultures, which will be addressed further below, Schein's statement again adds credence to a point made earlier, that much of the content we have been exploring connects up in interesting ways. Thus in understanding culture in an attempt to be better at doing our jobs and making decisions, we also better understand ourselves, a task we looked at in more detail in Chapter 2.

Getting to know a culture takes on a variety of different dimensions. It is common practice when applying for a job, for example, to go to an organization's website and read the mission statement, planning documents, etc. Certainly this is a good first step, but it really just scratches the surface when one considers the deeper implications of culture. Espoused beliefs, for example, through statements and interviews with managers and employees certainly dig a bit deeper. For building at least a minimal level of understanding about an organization's culture, it is necessary to talk with its members. The challenge, of course, as we have discussed before, is that espoused belief is not always the same as actual practice and behavior, so interviews coupled with observation give an even richer picture in this regard.

A number of other surface clues can also be informative to a limited degree. For example, physical space layout in a workplace can often provide clues about power, relationships, communication, etc. Understanding how people communicate in general is also critical. Do they communicate by e-mail, face to face, telephone, etc.? Do they have frequent meetings? If so, how are those meetings run? How do people dress? I served on one board which had monthly meetings, everyone was always very formally dressed and whoever was speaking was asked to stand at a podium. On another board upon which I served, meetings were bi-monthly, people dressed much more casually, seating was in a circle and people generally just spoke from their seat, interjecting as appropriate. The 'feel' of the two organizations, as one might suspect, was very different.

There are, beyond some of these more obvious ways of viewing an organization, a number of much more creative ways. One interesting way to learn about an organization is to mine commonly shared stories, especially those about a leader or those that in some way highlight a critical value of the organization. In my class I often ask students to share a story about a place they have worked that, to them, illustrates some aspect of the culture. For example, imagine a college campus where the president is very concerned about the physical plant and appearance. On such a campus, staff might tell stories about seeing the president walking the campus and bending down to pick up stray pieces of paper and/or rubbish on a regular basis. The message would be clear. We will take pride in the appearance of our campus. Similarly, imagine a campus dean who walks the campus on a daily basis and eagerly seeks out students and staff to speak with, dedicating as much as an hour to a random conversation about ideas or concerns. Again, another clear message is delivered: individual employees and students are important.

Several other creative ways exist to look at culture beyond stories like these. Oftentimes organizations have myths. These may even be taken from true stories, but exaggerated on a key element for emphasis. For example, one might exaggerate the story above to tell a newcomer to the organization that the president knows *every* student on campus personally. Surely this would be an impossible task at most, if not all, colleges, but it would deliver a message similar to the story mentioned above. Organizations may also have heroes or heroines who could reside in any position within an organization. For example, at a recent ceremony on our campus an award was given to a security officer. While many prestigious awards were given out, this was the only one which received a standing ovation. Why? The security officer grew suspicious when two students carried another student into the residence halls and the student being carried did not seem to be conscious. He immediately took action, calling 911. It was later determined that had he hesitated, the student would have died and he had, in fact, saved a life. Clearly, there could not be any greater assumption or cultural value for a university than taking responsibility for the safety of its students.

In this example of the security guard, there is yet another way to examine a culture. Virtually all cultures have rituals or ceremonies. The nature of these rituals and ceremonies often illustrates cultural assumptions and values in a number of ways. In the case mentioned above, the award was given as part of a larger awards ceremony held every year. A number of both real and joke awards are given at this ceremony. The real awards are decided upon by peer nomination and vote. The very process has cultural implications, as does who are chosen and the stated and unstated reasons why they are chosen to receive awards. Aside from larger and more formal rituals, one might ask what library staff do for an employee's birthday or to celebrate other important events in their lives. In my opinion, one of the most important rituals is to have a special get-together for those leaving the organization. While this provides an opportunity to share goodbyes and well-wishes, it also signifies the value we place on individuals and their success and happiness, even if it means we lost them to 'bigger and better things'.

Of course, much of what we have gone through here is still very superficial. According to Schein (ibid.: 112), understanding culture means digging deeper. Indeed, when viewed from the foundational and developmental perspective, he notes that important factors include 'Creating a common language and conceptual categories... Defining group boundaries and criteria for inclusion and exclusion... Developing norms of intimacy, friendship, and love... Defining and allocating awards and punishments... Explaining the unexplainable – ideology and religion...' Surely, all of these apply to libraries. Librarians as a subgroup actually share some common language and ideals; this will be discussed further below. Group boundaries may occur both around and within the library. Any library can have a more formal or perhaps a more collegial or even a family-like feel to it. Rewards and punishments are a part of any library job, even if they constitute something as a simple as a 'pat on the back' or a verbal reprimand. And if one digs deep enough, there is often an underlying reality or fundamental belief in the purpose of library services certainly shared by most, if not all, employees in a given library with a relatively stable culture.

Yet another much more limited but intriguing aspect of examining culture on a deeper level is exploring time orientation. Schein (ibid.: 152) suggests that different organizations have different time orientations. 'Cultural assumptions about time influence the role that planning will play in the management process.' What are the concerns on the minds of the library manager and library staff? Are they worried about how the reference desk or a library instruction session will be covered tomorrow? Are they concerned about establishing relationships with faculty, or collection development over the course of the coming year? Are they worried about the future of libraries in general, with tightening budgets and increasing costs of electronic resources? I would suggest, like most people, that there needs to be a balance. However, how that balance is created and where emphasis is placed may differ, certainly at different times but also on an ongoing basis from library to library.

Before closing out the topic, it is worth noting as an alternative framework Ronald Recardo and Jennifer Jolly's suggested dimensions for studying culture. According to Recardo and Jolly (1997: 8), all aspects of culture can be understood by exploring communications, training, rewards, how decisions are made, how risks are perceived, planning processes, how work teams interact and, among other aspects of leadership, 'how well management encourages diversity'.

We have only scratched the surface with this discussion of organizational culture, although hopefully we have covered enough to give some understanding of how it applies to libraries. With this understanding we can now further explore the separation of cultures or creation of subcultures, as well as other issues such as the process of socialization and how, as a library manager, one needs to be acutely aware of messages delivered as these relate to culture.

Subcultures

No library is an island unto itself. An academic library exists within a larger college or university. A school library is part of the school. A public library, while perhaps a bit more isolated, is still part of a broader array of public services and also often a larger library system. A law library is part of a bigger law firm, etc. This has serious implications for our discussion of culture. Organizational culture overlaps in ways similar to the way that our roles as individuals may overlap or even conflict. For example, one may be an employee of X university, a staff member in Y department, a member of Z profession, etc. An individual will also have a number of non-work roles, such as parent, friend, club member, etc., in which it could further be noted that the person may display different attributes. Likewise, when we speak about an organization's culture, we could be referring to a specific layer. For example, one might explore the organizational culture of the university, the library and the technical services department. What people refer to as 'us' and 'how we do things' may differ depending on the context and situation. The assumptions and values, and thus behavior, may line up well or could be entirely different as one moves through these different layers.

According to Schein (2004: 274), there are five typical layers or levels of subgroupings:

- functional/occupational differentiation
- geographical decentralization
- differentiation by product, market or technology
- divisionalization
- distinction by hierarchy.

Again, to bring this into the realm of the practical, some brief examples may be drawn out. A library manager has to consider occupational differences within the context of the broader organization. Librarians as a group would be expected to see the world in a slightly different way than, say, an admissions officer at a university. Geography is another critical factor. Many public library systems have branches that service very different patrons. Within some organizations, divisions exist that span geography: while geographically separated a library might be divisionally connected. For example, at Johnson & Wales University the libraries as a whole represent a division. While most planning occurs at a campus level, there is also planning and, most definitely, some shared culture/assumptions among the librarians in the institution as a division regardless of geographical location, in that we all essentially deliver a similar 'product'. Lastly, hierarchy plays a role in libraries as well. A library manager may share cultural assumptions as part of a broader group of library managers or managers within the organization in general. Sometimes the associated assumptions match those of the library subgroup and sometimes they may not.

While there is much to be said about the importance of libraries and library services, there is also a danger in strong and stable subgroups. According to Katz and Kahn (1966: 65), 'The tendency of any group of people occupying a given segment of an organization is to exaggerate the importance of their function and to fail to grasp the basic functions of the larger whole.' The warning here is never to forget that the library's goals and activities need to fit into a bigger and broader context. At a subgroup level, this is equally applicable. Technical services and reference services may have specialized functions, but the employees engaged in these areas need to appreciate their place in the wider institution or organization.

The socialization process

According to Katz and Kahn (ibid.: 304), the socialization process from an employee's perspective is 'to learn from the other members of the group how "things are really done," the unwritten but all important facts of organizational life'. As suggested by this statement, much of what goes into socialization is not part of the formal process of bringing one into a given organization. While there is a lot to this, other more formal aspects of socialization need not be entirely discounted. Libraries seem to be especially challenged in recognizing the importance of the socialization process. A recent study conducted and reported by Joanne Oud (2008) sought to uncover problems with socialization among new academic librarians in factors thought to impact on job satisfaction and turnover. Librarians' expectations differed considerably in a number of areas in terms of the incongruence between expectations accrued in the socialization process and what was actually expected of them in their jobs. For example, among other items, significant areas of difference included having much greater autonomy than expected, having a wider variety of responsibilities than expected, having to deal with bureaucracy on a regular basis, having to deal with 'slanted' views of the library from external parties and having little time for training. Oud further reports that some of the hardest things for librarians to learn were understanding the internal library politics, how to do collection development, understanding library procedures, dealing with conflict and building relationships with faculty. She points out how the comments on politics relate most closely with the broader issue, organizational culture, with which we are concerned. It is worth noting that some suggestions include more scheduled time for conversation with a supervisor and/or providing the librarian with an assigned mentor.

While there is good reason to heed Oud's advice and pay attention to aspects of socialization, it is also important to consider the critical issue of fit. It would be shortsighted for us not to discuss fit in relation to organizational culture. In their detailed investigation on the topic, Charles O'Reilly, Jennifer Chatman and David Caldwell highlight the presence of 'good fit' employees in organizations with stronger and more vibrant cultures. They note that 'results of a series of studies have shown that person-job fit predicts performance, satisfaction, and turnover across a variety of jobs' and that 'the congruency between an individual's values and those of an organization may be at the crux of person-culture fit' (O'Reilly et al., 1991: 491–2). Through an instrument which they created and utilized in their study, they were able to determine two years out that 'the degree to which individual preferences matched organizational realities was predictive of turnover two years later' (ibid.: 510). Their study also showed a significant connection to commitment and satisfaction over time. It is worth noting that their instrument, the OCP (organizational culture profile), consists of 'assessing attitudes toward, for instance, quality, respect for individuals, flexibility, and risk taking' (Chatman and Jehn, 1994: 529).

This study has some very important implications. Going back to the hiring issue, it is critically important to find individuals who will match well with the organization and to acculturate them properly. According to Schein (2004: 261), 'it is clear that initial selection decisions for new members, followed by the criteria applied in the promotion system, are powerful mechanisms for embedding and perpetuating the culture, especially when combined with socialization tactics designed to teach cultural assumptions'. This includes being as honest as possible in the interviewing process. It means that when a candidate asks a question, while the members of the organization want to put their best foot forward, so to speak, they also need to level with the candidate. For example, if professional development money will be hard to come by, don't gloss over it. If certain decisions will not be made democratically, don't pretend they will be. Honesty is critical. Beyond this, when we do make a decision to bring someone in, we need to address issues of fit continually. In some cases, where values are concerned, if a mismatch develops there is nothing that can be done but ultimately to effect a separation between employer and employee. A library manager might, however, have some flexibility in dealing with lesser incongruities. If a job can be crafted differently over time to make it a better fit, more productivity will result.

One of the foremost experts in describing the socialization process is John Van Maanen. He takes the view that socialization strategies are either consciously or unconsciously employed when we bring a new person into our organization. Usually, it is the latter of these. When people come into organizations, they experience anxiety about knowing what to do and how to behave, and so are highly motivated to learn. They look for cues from those around them to learn. And the effectiveness of an organization relies to a large extent upon how well new employees, in our case library employees, are socialized (Van Maanen, 1978).

Van Maanen posits that there are seven critical dimensions which need to be consciously considered when socializing a new employee, each of which we will address here very briefly.

Socialization may be a formal or informal process. That is, when a new librarian is hired, we may have a set plan for them to go through in order to learn about the organization. Conversely, we might just leave this largely up to chance. Like the other six dimensions, there can be aspects of both sides of this dimension in any give application. That is, a new librarian might go through a partially formalized socialization process alongside a partially informal process. The formal process places a bit more pressure on the employee to adapt and the informal process leaves a lot of power in the hands of the workgroup. If, for example, a manager had a number of employees committed to an older way of doing things and wanted change or had malcontents on the staff who could influence the new person, then informality could be a dangerous approach to take. On the other hand, if the manager felt confident that a positive ethic would be instilled by the workgroup, s/he might be more comfortable with a slightly more informal process (ibid.).

Another dimension is individual versus collective socialization. It is rare that libraries hire many librarians at once, but the latter would apply if this occurred. One side-effect of group socialization is a separate bonding among that group which occurs as they go through the socialization process together. Some variations of group socialization may exist as well. For example, a college campus might have periodic orientation days for groups of new employees whereby people from different departments come together to learn about core values. Thus a new librarian might participate in this process with a number of other new employees from admissions, student life, etc. (ibid.).

Sequential versus non-sequential is another dimension worthy of consideration. Again, in translating this dimension to libraries, it might involve consideration of whether or not a new librarian needs to receive an overview of access services before cataloging, for example, or if these can be scheduled in opposite order if more convenient (ibid.).

Yet another dimension is along the lines of fixed versus variable socialization. In a fixed schedule, for example, a new librarian might be told that they will not sit alone at the reference desk or perhaps engage in instruction on their own for x number of days. Conversely, in a variable approach they might simply do so when they feel comfortable and ready (ibid.).

One dimension which may not be particularly relevant to libraries is the tournament versus contest dimension. According to Van Maanen (ibid.), this approach centers on whether or not an individual can easily rise in an organization. Essentially, in a tournament model, once a determination is made that someone should go no further, they will never be considered for a higher-level position.

Another dimension is the serial versus disjunctive socialization process. This refers specifically to whether or not the new library staff member will be trained by the 'old hands' or more specifically by the person previously holding the job. Again, there are implications. If the manager seeks continuity, then having the person previously in the job spend time with the new person is beneficial. If, however, a change is sought, this approach would be detrimental (ibid.).

The last and perhaps most interesting dimension is the consideration of investiture versus divestiture. This relates to how much individuals will be encouraged to be themselves versus how much they will be expected to adapt to an organization. The question here becomes a matter of how great the need is on the part of the organization for one or the other. Harvard University's process of bringing on board new faculty would presumably be high in investiture and the US Army's approach in bringing in new recruits would be heavy on divestiture, for example (ibid.).

Maintaining and fostering change in organizational culture

The next question on our agenda is to consider how a library manager's behavior and communications may serve to stabilize and/or change organizational culture. There are two divergent reasons why library managers need to be aware of their impact. If the culture is strong and stable, the messages sent need to be congruent. If, on the other hand, change is necessary then a different approach may need to be consciously taken. Schein (2004) believes that managers act within a culture but leaders are needed to change it. Certainly, this points to the fact that in situations where a stable pre-existing organizational culture is in place, a manager simply manages it, and that to change an established and entrenched culture requires something more, something perhaps a bit special. In both cases, I would argue the most important component is self-awareness in both day-to-day and critical situations.

According to Schein (ibid.: 248), 'Some of the most important signals of what founders and leaders care about are sent during meetings and in other actions devoted to planning and budgeting, which is one reason why planning and budgeting are such important processes...' While his emphasis is on founders and leaders, we might hoist this statement on to all managers when they are engaged in these tasks. Clearly, the planning and budgeting processes have a fundamentally important relationship to vision and mission because they are the translation of these things. Both what a library manager pays attention to and doesn't pay attention to can say a lot. For example, a library manager might keep bringing the group back to discussions about information literacy or collections, indicating a clear point of emphasis that may be picked up by the group. In allocating funds, they also make it clear what matters most.

While budgeting and planning processes may occur only once a year, there are many other opportunities for a manager to communicate priorities and direct or support cultural assumptions. For example, one of the tools that a library manager has is the control of meeting agendas. While some aspects of a meeting's agenda may be left for the group to decide, the manager may also include specific points of emphasis. For example, an academic library director might decide to include an update on information literacy efforts in every staff or library committee meeting, signaling to everyone that this is an important topic which should always be at the forefront of efforts and activities. Another might be a campus-wide retention committee. A given campus or institution may have many committees, some more important than others. That said, in our example imagine this retention committee with representation from critical department heads. Imagine that the results achieved by the committee would be shared by the president whenever speaking to the faculty and staff as a group. And imagine as well that the findings and efforts of this group were included in all of the organization's publications. A message from the leadership is clear. At minimum, we need to keep our students to survive financially and, ideally, we are doing so by engaging them and constantly monitoring our efforts in this regard.

Another chance for a library manager to demonstrate what is important is in a crisis situation. With regard to the institutional entity itself, Schein (ibid.: 107) states: 'No one really knows what response it will make to a severe crisis, yet the nature of that response will reflect deep elements of the culture.' A crisis, in other words, is an opportunity. Picking up on a stream of recent news that runs through this book in its implications, the recent economic downturn has affected many libraries. How do we ultimately react to this? Do we hang our heads, refuse to make changes and cross our fingers, waiting for a miracle? Or is this a chance for a library manager to get staff together, evaluate the new circumstances and look at what options exist for moving forward? Again, for a concrete and practical example one could look at allocations on physical resources and determine if a shift towards more virtual resources might save money but expand access. Perhaps the very mission or goals of the library need to be reviewed, encouraging a creative response and change. In any case, doing something proactive and involving staff would be important. The message would be clear. We will adapt, survive and thrive. In a broader sense, Roxanne Selberg (2009: 13), in her recent discussion of leading cultural change in libraries, included a subheading which reads 'Be the change you want to see'. That is, if behavioral change is sought, it should begin with the library manager. It is also worth noting her emphasis on open discussion, allowing everyone, especially on cross-functional teams, to share their concerns about challenges and changes. Only in unearthing the assumptions can the need for change be met head on.

In closing, we will go back to organizational culture guru Edgar Schein one more time. He suggests that the ultimate culture to which we should aspire is what he calls the learning culture. This certainly applies to libraries. We need to be proactive, committed to learning and understand that we can't control everything in the external environment. We also need to focus more on the future and think more systematically. According to Schein (2004: 398), 'The only way to build a learning culture that continues to learn is for leaders themselves to realize that there is much that they do not know and must teach others to accept that there is much that they do not know. The learning task then becomes a shared responsibility.'

Thoughts for consideration or discussion

- What is the culture like where you work now or where you have worked in the past?
- What stories could you tell about a job or jobs that you have held which would demonstrate some aspect of the culture (good or bad)?
- How is your behavior affected by the culture of your workplace or an organization to which you belong?
- What would an ideal academic, public or school library culture to work in look like?

- How were you socialized in your current job or a previous job which you held?
- What would an ideal socialization process in an academic, public or school library look like?

Case study: Mary wants to hear... or does she?

Mary, the library director, walked into the boardroom and noted that they were going to start the meeting immediately. Sitting around the room were the senior staff of Large Public Library. To start things off, Mary asked everyone to consider ideas for bolstering library usage, which had dropped off considerably of late. Although she expressed an interest in 'hearing all ideas', when Joanne shared hers Mary said that it was entirely impractical. Next, Mark shared his thoughts, to which Mary answered back with sarcasm. Meanwhile, the more veteran staff remained silent and just shrugged their shoulders. They all thought the same thing: 'Why doesn't she just tell us what she already wants to do and get it over with?'

- What kinds of messages came across in this short encounter? Did they conflict?
- Assuming we are seeing typical behavior and interactions, what does this indicate about the culture in this library?

Case study: Lisa learns her way

Joanne was excited. As a high-school librarian at a school as small as this one, one doesn't always get an assistant, but the principal was allowing her to hire one. It was, after all, a formal preparatory school where parents paid good money to have their children enrolled. She felt that they should get top-notch resources and services. Joanne, attired as she was in professional dress, couldn't help but notice what Lisa was wearing when she strolled in for her first day of work: a pair of jeans and sneakers. She made a mental note right away to talk about the issue of dress with her, which she did later in the day. After getting settled in, they began chatting. Lisa asked Joanne what the principal, Mr Manning, was like. Joanne commented that he was great but added, 'Just make sure you look busy when he comes in. He doesn't like us to be not busy. At one point a few years ago, he saw us as "not busy" and talked about reducing my position to half-time.' She went on: 'He really is a great principal, just as long as you don't get on his bad side.'

Later, at lunchtime, Joanne asked Lisa to join her in the faculty lounge. As they sat to eat, Joanne was unexpectedly called away. One of the teachers, however, came in, introduced herself as Julie and sat down with Lisa. Over lunch Julie decided to fill Lisa in: 'Watch out for Mr Grimm. He's the music teacher and he hits on everyone. I'm sure you already heard about our principal. Well, watch out for his office assistant, Susie, too. She reports everything to him. I am sure that Joanne told you as well, but in addition to her you can always go to the vice principal, Mr McGregor, if you have a problem. You can always hang out with us to get more of the scoop. A bunch of us usually go out for happy hour at TGI Fridays once a month.'

Later, Joanne came by and they went back to the library. At about 3.15 pm, Joanne asked Lisa if she wanted to leave for the day. Lisa was puzzled, as she thought that she was expected to work until 4 pm every day. Joanne responded: 'Mr Manning has already left by now. He usually goes early on Tuesdays. No harm in leaving a little early. Besides, there aren't any books to reshelve and we'll have plenty of time in the morning to pick up where we started.'

- What has Lisa learned in her first day of work?
- What might it be like to work here?
- Do we get a hint of some of the relationships?

Project ideas

- Using the criteria discussed in this chapter, describe the organizational culture of a particular library. You might do this by both observation and interviews with library staff. The following questions may help as guidelines:

   1. Does the library support the professional growth of its employees? If so, how?

   2. How high is the turnover?

   3. What is the dominant leadership style?

4. How is employee morale?

5. How do people dress?

6. How are the public spaces and offices arranged? How about break rooms, etc.?

7. What is the length of the normal workday?

8. How do people communicate?

9. What is the library director like? If it's a bigger library, how about other library administrators?

10. What are the espoused values of the library (e.g. mission statement, etc.)?

11. Are there any stories that are told to illustrate the library's culture? Is there any particular hero or heroine?

12. What rituals are in place? What is the importance of these rituals?

13. How are people rewarded for doing a good job (or are they?)?

14. How are decisions made: top down, by an individual, by certain groups...?

15. Is the culture more formal, easygoing or a mix of the two?

16. Are there any logos or symbols the organization uses? What do these signify?

17. Are formal reviews of employees done on an annual basis? What type of process is in place for this?

18. How are new people hired? How are they then socialized? How does one get promoted?

19. What does the library spend its money on?

20. Is the library diverse?

21. What is the typical level of education among library employees? Are there mostly librarians? Do the staff consist of a mix of professionals and paraprofessionals, etc.?

■ Go to Van Maanen's (1978) original article and answer the following questions about workplace socialization either alone or in a group. What is the central tenet of John Van Maanen's article?

1. What are his three assumptions?

2. What are the seven dimensions?

3. What is the purpose of formal versus informal socialization? Which typically comes first?

4. If a *laissez-faire* approach is taken to training, what will take on greater influence according to Van Maanen?

5. What are the differences between individual and group socialization?

6. What are the differences between sequential and non-sequential socialization? What about Van Maanen's view that different agents in the process can have different approaches and agendas to what is important? Does this occur in the MLIS program – is it a strength or a weakness? What kind of pressure might exist in a workplace with sequential socialization?

7. What are the differences between fixed and variable strategies? What are the positives of the fixed? In the variable does this mean that individuals have no idea of when the next step might come?

8. What is tournament socialization and what are its negative effects?

9. What is the difference between serial and disjunctive socialization? What might the differences be between taking over an old established library with staff who had been in their role for a long time versus setting up one that was brand new?

10. Could teachers be socialized by students? How?

11. How do the investiture and divestiture approaches differ? Van Maanen claims that professors must 'suffer' something akin to divestiture. How about librarians?

5

Communication

When it comes to management and the broader topic of leadership (addressed more completely in the next chapter), few, if any, issues are more important than communication. According to Deborah Barrett (2006: 385), 'Managers spend most of their day engaged in communication...' She goes on to highlight older studies indicating that, even before e-mail and cell phones, somewhere between 70 per cent and 90 per cent of a manager's daily work involved communicating in some fashion (ibid.).

It should be noted that this chapter takes a slightly different approach from some of the earlier ones. While there is a solid foundation of theory that applies to communicating, an attempt has been made here to be as practicable as possible. Hence the chapter has been organized around the various ways in which managers and others communicate. An attempt has also been made to incorporate some practical scholarship on best practices in these situations.

Fundamentals of communication

According to Barrett (ibid.: 386), 'Communication is the transmission of meaning from one person to another or to many people, whether verbally or non-verbally.'

Communication typically begins with the encoding of a message. By encoding, we are referring to the way in which a given person chooses to communicate and the fact that their message is essentially crafted out of the totality of their experiences, as well as how they view the world. The second component in communicating is transmission. This specifically refers to the means by which the person who encodes the message chooses to deliver it. Means of transmission vary considerably, and will be discussed in detail below. The next component in communicating is decoding. This refers to how a message is understood at the other end. Because decoding also involves interpretation based on one's unique experiences, communicating may be viewed as a fairly complex process with serious potential challenges. In the words of one author, 'A receiver who has a similar frame of reference to that of the sender will experience less difficulty in decoding than one whose frame of reference differs considerably. One of the major challenges of communicating globally is developing common frames of reference and bridging cultural difference' (Gordon, 2002: 219). Lastly, feedback refers to the decoder's acknowledgment of the receipt of a message, and the process by which the encoder can determine whether or not the decoder has understood what was intended (ibid.).

Traditional ways of communicating

Face-to-face discussion or communication, the most traditional of all forms of communicating, remains a vital avenue for developing connections and sharing information in the modern library workplace. According to a recent study, 75 percent of the business executives queried indicated that in-person communication was the most effective means of communicating with employees (*OfficePro*, 2007). As with all aspects of communication discussed here, level and frequency of contact may vary considerably when we examine face-to-face communications between a leader/manager and employees in a given context. For example, a library director responsible for 120 employees will probably not have a lot of face-to-face meetings with the vast majority of them, but may spend considerable time with a handful of direct subordinates who, in turn, spend time with other managers and employees. A manager of a department within a library or a director at a small library may, on the other hand, spend considerable time communicating directly with each employee who reports to him or her.

The advantages of face-to-face communication are considerable. While we will address several of the more common ways for communicating in the workplace, direct one-to-one communication clearly stands head and shoulders above the others in several ways. Most importantly, it allows an individual to interpret and utilize a more full range of communication possibilities. The specific ability to incorporate non-verbal aspects is the reason why face-to-face communication is so rich in terms of possibility. In one study, 94 percent of individuals queried 'felt that nonverbal communication in the business world was either somewhat or very important' (Graham et al., 1991: 46). Library studies, especially those which examine reference services, seem to concur. For example, in one study patrons' perceptions were explored regarding their willingness to approach the reference desk. The study found that, of the five categories into which comments were later grouped, four related to non-verbal communication (Radford, 1998).

What exactly do we mean by non-verbal communication? It is a fairly broad term and encompasses a number of different things. Some of the most frequently noted items are eye contact, facial expression and handshakes (ibid.; Graham et al., 1991; Hiemstra, 1999). In terms of facial expression, I was recently struck by a scene in *Last Chance Harvey* when Dustin Hoffman is speaking with Emma Thompson. Without saying a word, her expression changes and he says, 'You just got sad.' Despite her upbeat musings to that point in time, he knew in an instant, by her expression, that something had changed (Hopkins, 2009). In one of the earlier landmark studies on non-verbal communication, Albert Mehrabian and Morton Wiener reported that tone of voice is actually more critical than what is said. According to Mehrabian and Wiener (1967: 113), 'the tonal component makes a disproportionately greater contribution to the interpretation of the total message than does the content component'. Beyond these elements, non-verbal communication can encompass everything from body posture to relative positioning and movement. Michael McCaskey (1979) goes so far as to include the set-up of office furniture. For example, speaking to someone from behind one's desk has different implications than sitting with them at a round table.

For a manager, non-verbal communication is critical on a number of levels. It is important both to send congruent signals relative to the verbal messages which you deliver and also to be able to interpret when an incongruent message has been received, especially from a supervisor or direct subordinate. As stated earlier in this book, it is critical to get to know one's subordinates, supervisor and other key stakeholders in the library. One necessary skill for a library manager is to be able to tell when someone's words do not match their non-verbal communication. Think of a case, for example, when someone is having a conflict or challenge and responds that 'everything is fine', and yet their non-verbal communication indicates anything but. It may be important to probe further in cases such as these to see what kind of a challenge, for example, an employee may be facing. Or, in the case of one's boss, it may be important to push (gently) for concerns he or she has about a given topic or issue under discussion or consideration. On both fronts, sometimes people try to bury concerns for a whole variety of reasons, only for them to resurface and become bigger problems later. The important thing is to be able to get others to open up and communicate as fully and meaningfully as possible.

On the opposite side, as encoder, it is also very important for one to be able to convey the proper messages. It has been at least hinted at above that we show our true selves through our non-verbal communication. It should be noted that controlling one's message in this area can be very difficult. To some extent, it goes back to Daniel Goleman's points on emotional intelligence, and more specifically the ability to exercise self-control. That said, nobody will be able consistently to deliver messages they do not believe in without giving off tell-tale signs. In fact, this is the premise of a TV show on Fox, 'Lie to Me'. For a manager, it means that when you deliver a tough or critical message, it is important to bring yourself around to developing congruency with that message. In some cases, for example, a manager may need to deliver a message on a policy that he or she doesn't agree with. In this case it is better for the manager to focus on facts (i.e. this needs to get done this way and it will get done this way) as opposed to feelings. Focusing on feelings will only send mixed messages, in that one's non-verbal communication may not match what is being said. There is something to be said here for honesty as well.

In-person meetings facilitate the use of non-verbal communication, which helps immediate encoding, transmission, decoding and feedback. If run properly, they may also create greater group cohesion, understanding and purpose. Unfortunately, meetings seem to be an especially tough challenge for managers. Some superficial evidence of this can be seen in the titles of books such as *Death by Meeting: A Leadership Fable – About Solving the Most Painful Problem in Business* by Patrick Lencioni (2004) or chapter headings such as 'Not another meeting' in *Meetings Made Easy: The Ultimate Fix-It Guide* (Micale, 2004: 1). Other authors write about poorly planned and run meetings where people get together simply because they have set up a system that they will meet at a certain time (even if there is no real purpose) or hold meetings where people simply talk past each other and waste time (Bassett, 2005; Fabian, 1995).

A number of elements go into making a meeting successful and capitalizing on the rich possibilities that this form of communicating has to offer. Most fundamentally, experts agree that the general purpose of the meeting needs to be considered. Two types seem to predominate. One might have weekly meetings that are informative sessions in which updates are shared across the team or workgroup. This type of meeting, generally speaking, lends itself well to being rather brief. Another broad area is meetings that require brainstorming and/or incorporate group planning processes. These would generally be longer and have a somewhat different tone to them.

When setting up a meeting for either purpose, its success will depend on preparation. An appropriate agenda, which includes rough time allocations for various items, should be set, especially for the quick-update type of meeting. A determination also needs to be made as to who the appropriate participants will be. Micale (2004: 3) additionally suggests establishing a 'meeting outcome statement', by which she means a written statement that indicates what is expected to be accomplished at the meeting (even if it is only sharing knowledge or understanding across departments). Another useful item to consider beforehand is whether or not participants will need to be familiar with specific documents or information. If so, these should be sent far enough in advance of the meeting for them to be reviewed.

In conducting the meeting, one needs to stay focused and alert. One study indicated that the biggest frustration *by far* that people have with meetings is 'drifting off subject' (Haynes, 1997: 6). Micale emphasizes the need in informational meetings to keep to a strict timetable and move things along. A major point also made by Micale regarding brainstorming and planning meetings is that one should actually draw out conflict. The very point of these meetings is to explore views and ideas that may be lingering beneath the surface. She states, 'There is value in allowing everyone to struggle at important decision points' (Micale, 2004: 27). The manager needs, however, to be sure that he or she still manages the group's discussion. Dominant participants may need to be dealt with and shy participants may need to be drawn out (ibid.). Haynes (1997) agrees with many of these points but adds the need to institute a process for actually evaluating the effectiveness of meetings. This can be done in the form of a simple questionnaire provided to participants.

Almost any library manager will, at some point, need to facilitate meetings. They could be meetings of a small workgroup, an entire library staff (in a smaller library), a library committee including faculty or teachers, a cross-functional committee involving multiple employees from areas outside the library, etc. In all cases, the advice provided above applies. Of course, meetings may also occur in a number of other formats, such as conference calls or video-conferencing. While these may lack access to some of the non-verbal cues discussed, many of the rules, such as staying on track, keeping people focused and making sure there is balance in participation, will apply.

Before moving on to newer forms of communicating that have become and/or are becoming more prevalent, it is worth exploring the one traditional means of communication that utilizes technology: telephones. While phone use may now mean anything from a traditional land-line to a cell tower or voice over internet protocol, the pros and cons remain the same. The biggest advantage of telephone communication over face to face, of course, is the ability to overcome distance. The distance could be anything from speaking to a librarian on the other side of the world to facilitate research on the part of a faculty member to communicating an urgent matter with the principal, whose office may be located just down the hall. Generally speaking, telephone communication has become cheap and easy. It offers some of the big advantages of face-to-face communication in being both synchronous and allowing for at least some non-verbal communication to be factored in (either by voice inflection or, in video-conferencing, in actually being able to see the other individual). Like face-to-face communication, it shares the challenge of typically being more time consuming than sending a quick e-mail message. Also, while the two parties may not need to be physically present with one another, they still must both be on the phone at the same time. While active listening will be discussed in more detail below, one of its basic premises, the need to focus one's attention, is very important in telephone conversations. Not only can we learn from our own profession in terms of telephone reference, but from other professions as well. For example, Sabena Jameel (2008) counsels medical doctors to pay close attention when taking consults by phone, in addition to tuning out background distractions, listening carefully to understand a patient's emotional state and probing for any hidden information.

The telephone can be a great tool for communicating as a library manager. As has been stated earlier, a typical library director, for example, spends an inordinate amount of time both reading and sending e-mail messages. Not only can a phone conversation add the elements mentioned above, it can facilitate a more effective and efficient resolution to a problem. One might find oneself e-mailing back and forth, for example, with a human resources department manager, answering and asking simple questions. We become so habituated to our use of e-mail until it finally occurs to us just to pick up the phone and spend a few moments coming to a resolution on a particular problem or issue. Another of the biggest advantages of the phone over e-mail is that it is much less likely to lead to misinterpreted communication, especially in terms of its emotional component. Time and again individuals in the workplace send messages that come across wrong. Think about getting an e-mail message that says, 'NO, that's not what I wanted!'; without even having a context to place this in, what is your reaction? Then consider someone making a quick phone call and, in a patient and friendly voice, saying 'Hi. I just thought I'd call because that's not what I wanted. Could I instead have...' In most cases, the latter approach would be more effective in gaining your cooperation, right?

New ways of communicating

By far the most widely used 'newer' method of communicating is e-mail. Obviously, its use having been widespread for most of the past two decades, it is hardly 'brand new'. Still, it seems that we have yet fully to come to grips with e-mail communication. Any search for information on this topic will lead one to scores of articles on how 'evil' e-mail is, or at least how difficult and challenging it is to manage. As a result, some companies have resorted to 'no e-mail Fridays' and other ways to contain its use. According to one author, 'New research indicates that over-reliance on e-mail can degrade an organization's interpersonal communications' (Wellner, 2005: 37). Still, as mentioned earlier, handling e-mail is a major part of any academic library director's job. This is probably true for many, if not most, other library positions as well. E-mail is a very important means of communicating for any library manager, and so its use needs to be considered carefully. According to Carl Evans and Warren Wright (2008: 24), 'when emails are sent almost automatically, without initially considering whether they should be sent or not, or whether other means of communication would be more effective, then problems start to occur'.

When sending e-mail, it has become increasingly important to be able both to limit the volume that we send and to be as succinct as possible in terms of content. Directional avenues of communication (e.g. communication to one's boss versus one's direct subordinates) will be discussed further below in terms of some dissimilarities; however, it should be noted that many similarities exist as well. For example, if you were to send your supervisor, direct subordinates or other colleagues within your organization too many e-mails, they might begin to tune out your messages. It is not much different to the boy who cried wolf. When you really have something important to share, it could get lost in the pile. Likewise, if you can condense a message, even if it takes time to do so, it is worth the effort. In my earliest days as library director, I had a habit of sending both long and overly frequent e-mails to faculty. When I went to the academic dean lamenting how I was getting little communication back from the faculty about various initiatives, he suggested that I both cut back and make more succinct my communication to them. While it remains a challenge at times to get faculty to respond to some communication efforts, the level of engagement was improved when I implemented these changes. Librarians are particularly susceptible to these drawbacks regarding e-mail for two reasons: we are passionate about what we do, and we tend to pay close attention to a mind-numbing array of details. One last piece of advice from Doug Bezier (2007) is worth sharing. Pay attention to your use of subject headings for messages and how you sculpt the text (e.g. using features such as bullet points, bold text, etc.).

Much has been said about the various ways in which e-mail gets slopped around. This too needs to be addressed. There are, indeed, many times when it is appropriate to 'cc' others on a given communication. For example, if a branch library director was facing a problem and discussing that problem with another branch library director, and he or she felt that a third branch director could be facing the same challenge, it is sensible and efficient to include them in the conversation. As another example, if a library director is communicating something about an issue to a specific library department chair, such as head of reference, and knows that the head of technical services will potentially be affected by the response, he or she might be included. There really are numerous situations in which it is useful to include others in an e-mail message. That having been said, there are also occasions on which it is either inefficient or even inappropriate to do so.

One e-mail item that is just a complete no-brainer is *never* to send overly emotional messages or messages that directly criticize others by e-mail unless you are ready to have a much wider audience see them. You never know when someone is going to click the forward button and send your message along or respond and 'cc' someone else. While some authors have harped on the legal risks associated with e-mail messages, the bottom line is that, even if you don't open yourself to a libel suit, you can very easily damage relationships (Mancini, 2006). Thus you need to think carefully before sending. This goes for staff as well as managers.

Sometimes a manager will be required to explain to staff what kinds of messages are or are not appropriate to send by e-mail and, as noted in an earlier chapter, this, along with all ways of communicating, can be determined in large part by the library's unique culture. A somewhat less egregious tendency by some is to include too little or too few people in a given e-mail thread. I've seen instances where individuals have been justifiably frustrated or angered by being left out of a discussion relevant to their job responsibilities. Likewise, some individuals include too many others. I remember a library organization that I was a part of having a discussion about giveaways at a workshop. The discussion included somewhere in the neighborhood of a couple of dozen separate e-mails sent to everyone's inbox to determine a simple giveaway!

Despite all its drawbacks, e-mail probably still reigns as the king of communication in libraries. It holds this position because, when used appropriately, it is very efficient. It allows an individual to communicate very quickly and, on the other end, the recipient to respond at a time that is convenient for them. As a library director, I could not imagine being able to balance and maintain all the communication that I need to engage in without such a tool.

Another tool for communicating is the library's website. While a library manager will not typically use a website for day-to-day communication, its use and importance need to be considered. From the perspective of many patrons, the website is the library! Thus a consistent message needs to be crafted. With websites, this message includes design elements as well. What does your library stand for? What services does it wish to highlight? Inevitably, choices must be made, and these choices will convey a message.

Blogs are yet another tool in what seems to be an ever-expanding retinue. In my library, the use of a blog has come to replace what was once a library newsletter. Instead of publishing information about the library once a month, it can now be published as necessary. Furthermore, it is a more open system which allows people outside the library to comment. The drawback is that, in some cases, blogs often do not receive much traffic. A recent study conducted at Boise State University showed all too typical results in this regard. After launching blogs with much fanfare, the authors noted, 'After one year, a review of the blogs was undertaken to assess their effectiveness as an outreach tool to faculty. Using the Google Analytics tool, it was determined that faculty readership of the blogs was minimal to nonexistent' (Kozel-Gains and Stoddart, 2009: 133). This doesn't bode well, but doesn't justify giving up either. It could signify the need for the library to publicize blogs better, or even faculty demographics to change as more and more from Generation Y are recruited to teaching.

Yet another approach to communicating which has caught on is social networking. In higher education, sites such as Facebook seem to predominate. These sites allow all sorts of connections between individuals and can open the door to newfangled marketing opportunities for libraries. While academic libraries still seem to be struggling to utilize these networks to their advantage (it seems that many college students prefer to keep these social networks as 'non-academic' as possible), public libraries have had some success, particularly when it comes to promoting specific programming in the library. According to Melanie Wood, a librarian at Morrison Public Library in Charlotte, NC, Facebook has been extremely helpful in raising program awareness and attendance. Social networking sites such as Facebook or Twitter are, indeed, intriguing for their possibilities, but they also come with some serious challenges. Much has been made recently about inappropriate postings. For example, a teacher in Charlotte, NC, lost her job as a result of an especially foolish posting on Facebook (Helms, 2008). When one considers how a US Supreme Court justice, Sonia Sotomayor, was 'grilled' in confirmation hearings in 2009 over one statement made many years earlier, one might also consider the impact of a permanent digital record of thoughts and musings as encouraged by Facebook and other social networking sites. Again, it may be okay to flirt with a little eccentricity in posts (e.g. I often post my thoughts about the latest games played by the New England Patriots and comment respectably on various news stories), and there are some amazing possibilities for communicating in general (e.g. we once used Facebook to let people know the library would be open even though the campus network was temporarily down), but there are also potential dangers.

With all of the emerging technologies working their way into libraries, there are many less-utilized avenues which will not be discussed here. Still, a passing mention should be made of wikis. These have become more and more popular in the library workplace for a wide variety of reasons. They can be used to share information with outside entities, but may also be used for internal information. For example, this kind of tool lends itself well towards being utilized in place of an employee handbook. Important policy and procedural information can be shared across a workgroup or a library through a well-designed wiki. They may also be used for projects. According to one source, the consequence of their increased usage has led to 'the emergence of a more collaborative organizational culture' (*Strategic Direction*, 2009: 21).

Listening

Moving away from the various means by which information is transmitted between the encoder and decoder, special attention needs to be paid to how we listen. Listening skills are critically important for any library manager, and for any librarian working in a public service area as well. In our modern desire to multitask, it can require a significant amount of discipline for us to focus on this very important task when necessary. What does active and effective listening look like? According to Micale (2004), we need to use non-verbal means of acknowledgment, rephrase the responses or statements of others and not be afraid to show empathy in our interactions with others. In the simplest sense, active listening boils down to one thing: be there. There is an excellent video which I often show my class, entitled *Fish: Catch the Energy, Release the Potential!*; it highlights the work culture at the Pike's Place fish market in Seattle, WA. In describing their approach to customer service, they emphasize the need to be present at all times (Christensen, 2002). In a practical sense, this may mean that a library manager needs to recognize times when an employee needs more focused attention. In such cases, scheduling an appointment for when undivided attention may be given is entirely appropriate.

Directional communication

Something needs to be said here about directional communication. As stated above, there are many similarities in how to approach communicating depending upon the audience. In the case of one's boss, one must understand his or her unique needs and challenges. One needs to balance keeping the boss informed and not becoming overly demanding of the person's limited time. When someone is working with a new supervisor, this is something that will have to be worked out over time. Other personality characteristics come into play as well. If the supervisor prefers detail, then by all means provide it. If, however, they prefer information to come in broad strokes, you should attempt to adapt your style accordingly.

When working with direct subordinates, an understanding of them as individuals is equally important; however, one might have a greater ability to craft communication along the lines that the library manager sees as most effective. Much will be said about setting an example in the final chapter on leadership. The way that a manager chooses to communicate with staff will also provide a powerful message to them as to how they, in turn, should communicate with him or her and how they should communicate among themselves. One especially important aspect of communicating with staff is the need to serve as a conduit for information. Often senior staff are privy to organization-wide information that may not have filtered down to other staff. Thus being a source for providing that information is a major function of any manager. This can be both difficult and rewarding, depending on circumstances. Sometimes it is good news that can be passed along; other times, the news may be related to a difficulty or challenge that lies ahead. In the case of the latter, as mentioned earlier, one needs to think through carefully the best way to convey such a message. One last point is worth making with regard to communicating with one's staff. Sometimes we are told of the need to stay aloof. According to Buckingham and Coffman (1999: 202), however, when this question is put to them: 'The most effective managers say yes, you should build personal relationships with your people, and no, familiarity does not breed contempt.'

Communicating laterally is a particularly interesting facet of communication to consider, especially since, aside from library managers communicating with other library managers, it often means interacting with others in the organization who think and communicate very differently to librarians. One of the greatest recommendations I can make in this regard is not only to get to know, for example in a university environment, other department heads, but also to stretch your boundaries and involvement to improve your interactions outside the library. My experience on non-profit boards and involvement in training with non-library folks has been extraordinarily helpful in this regard. If we can learn to see the world the way others outside of our profession do, we can be much more influential in getting our message across and our goals accomplished.

Before moving on, it is worth sharing some formal means by which lateral communication works within my organization. At Johnson & Wales University's Charlotte campus, the library director is involved in several committees to a greater or lesser degree: the Library & Information Literacy Committee, Deans' Council, Operations Council, Arts & Sciences Events Planning Committee, Retention Advisory

Committee, Information Technology Services Committee, Directors' Committee/Meetings, etc. By staying active in these groups, communication flows regularly both to and from the library.

Lastly, when considering special groups, one needs to consider how to communicate with patrons. As stated earlier, outside people will often come to view the library manager or director as the library itself. While a manager may bring hard and tough truths to the attention of staff or a supervisor, communicating with the public should always be framed in a positive way. This extends to the broader organization of which the manager may be a part. When serving on the board of a typical non-profit organization, one is regularly reminded of the need to be able to give the 'one-minute elevator speech', for example. This may include something about the mission of the organization and a hook or event that the person spoken to might wish to know about. Likewise, the library manager should always be prepared. Marketing and promoting the library's use, whether to faculty and students or to a broader community, are a major function of any library manager. Thus maintaining an appropriate professional appearance and communicating in a professional way are critical. This cannot be overstated.

Networking

Before closing out this chapter, we touch on the need for a manager to pay attention to networking. Fred Luthans (1988) explored the difference between successful versus effective managers. He found that a manager's effectiveness could be determined by the amount of quality time they spent with staff. The success of managers in terms of promotions, however, correlated with the amount of external networking they did. According to Luthans (ibid.: 130), 'we found that networking makes the biggest relative contribution to manager success'. Of course, it is worth noting that Luthans is disturbed by the finding that effectiveness does not necessarily lead to success. Thus managers who work very hard with their staff and with their nose to the grindstone may not be rewarded. The conclusion which should be drawn from this study, however, is the need to pay attention to both the internal needs of employees and outside networking opportunities. Much is to be said, especially in libraries, about how managers actively engaged in external networking are better positioned to import new ideas into the organization, to find opportunities for external cooperation and partnerships and to open doors and opportunities not just for oneself, but for one's staff as well. Luckily, librarians tend to be very actively engaged in professional associations, such as their local or state library organization and/or the American Library Association. The ALA's Library Leadership and Management Association offers some of the best opportunities for library managers or aspiring library managers in this regard.

Thoughts for consideration or discussion

- Can you think of instances in communicating with someone when their non-verbal communication, such as facial expression or voice tone, did not match their words? What were the circumstances?

- What is the worst meeting you have ever been to, and why was it so bad?

- What is the best meeting you have ever been to, and why was it so good?

- Have you ever sent an e-mail that you wish you hadn't sent?

- Have you ever received an e-mail that you felt was unprofessional or inappropriate?

- Do you think about how you communicate with your present boss or a past supervisor? What kinds of things did you consider?

- What experience do you have with social networking? If you have a social networking page, what kind of posts do you put on it?

- How would you dress or present yourself if you were speaking to the community and representing the local public library?

- What kinds of networking-related activities do you engage in? What other opportunities might you consider now or in the future?

Case study: she said what!? ...to whom!?

In June, Kate had been hired as the new reference librarian at Small Valley Community College. As part of her job, Kate also had some instruction responsibilities. Robert, her manager and the library director, spent a significant amount of time with Kate over the summer going through what she needed to know. As part of her socialization process, she was encouraged to engage in open discussion about reference and instruction-related issues with the rest of the staff. Before the school year began, a plan was made to facilitate instruction by borrowing a laptop and projector from the information technology services (ITS) department in order to do library instruction in the classrooms (as opposed to the library computer lab where it had been done before). While all classrooms had network lines installed, most did not have computers and so the portable laptop was necessary.

Shortly into the school year, it became apparent that the new approach was not working. Despite making reservations with ITS well in advance, the librarians responsible for instruction frequently found that either a laptop and/or a projector was unavailable when they were supposed to go into a class or they didn't work properly (e.g. access to the desktop was locked out, the network line didn't seem to work, connection to the overhead projector didn't work, etc.).

As a result of the problems, Robert took several steps. First, he met face to face with the manager of the ITS department. In a nutshell, the response was agreement that they were having problems, but that they were understaffed and were working with old equipment. They were simply doing 'the best they could' and there should not be an expectation that things would change in the short term. Long-term prospects were much better, but this would take time. The second step that Robert took was to talk with the dean about allowing the library to use funds that were allocated to collection development, so the library could buy some equipment of its own (i.e. a laptop and projector). The dean explained that it was not institutional policy to allow this and the library would have to continue to rely upon ITS for the equipment. The third and final step taken by Robert was to bring the library staff together to meet and discuss the problem. At this meeting everyone was asked to share their views and consider possible solutions. In the end, the group decided that it would be better to go back to the old model of using the library computer lab when possible for instruction sessions and no longer attempt to utilize the unreliable equipment. This would be done with the understanding that it could be tried again in the future.

The next day, Kate e-mailed the director of ITS, the director of facilities and the academic dean. In her e-mail, she stated that the idea that the library would no longer go to the classes was 'stupid'. Furthermore, she insinuated that the rest of the library staff and possibly

ITS staff were incompetent, and that this is why the problem existed. She offered no particular solution but just wanted 'her voice to be heard'.

After receiving the message, the academic dean called Robert and asked to speak with him in person. He showed him the e-mail and asked him what he intended to do about it. Specifically, he noted, 'Her way of communicating here is entirely inappropriate.' Robert acknowledged the dean's observation and also felt slightly shocked, since he thought he had given ample opportunity in the meeting for Kate to have raised her concerns with the library group instead of airing them to those outside the group.

- What does Robert need to do?
- How could Kate have done things differently?
- What could Robert do in the future to avoid this kind of internal library challenge?
- What can and/or should Robert do in terms of communicating on the problem itself with the rest of the academic community (for example, how would faculty be told about the change)?

Case study: they posted what!?

Mary was excited. She was finally going to get a Facebook account. As the library director at a small public library in Massachusetts, Brady Public Library (BPL), she had not yet had a chance to get involved in online social networking. Recently, however, one of her newest librarians had convinced her that the library could promote itself through a Facebook page and that her involvement would be both necessary and fun. As a result, this staff member had created the library fan page and most of the staff had scrambled either to create accounts or to link up with one another online.

A few days after signing on and sending out friend requests to several staff who she knew were on Facebook, Mary logged in to find out that she had, in fact, some new friends. As she began to poke around on various people's pages, however, she was troubled by what she saw. Patricia was one of the library's paraprofessional staff members. On Patricia's page she saw an old status update that read 'Patricia is sick of dealing with so many dumb patrons.' As she kept clicking, she came across the page of Michael, one her reference librarians. On the wall located on Michael's page was a comment by Joanne. It read, 'Hey,

Michael, I am glad to be here in Facebook finally. I wonder if we will ever get rid of that idiot director of ours. Could you believe that meeting today!?' Joanne was another librarian at BPL who had not accepted Mary's friend request. Finally, she came across another staff member's page. Lisa was a younger reference librarian who had obviously been on Facebook for quite a long time. On her page, she explained why her last relationship had ended. She went into great detail, both naming her ex-boyfriend and stating his faults one by one (including his medical history and ability as a lover).

Mary was no longer as excited as she had been about entering Web 2.0. She had heard so much about these online forums and their positive aspects. What was she to make of what she was seeing here?

- Does Mary need to address any general issues regarding the staff relating to online social networking?

- Does Mary need to speak with Patricia, Joanne and/or Lisa? If so, what should she say?

- Does Mary still push forward in her support for the library having a presence on Facebook?

Case study: who is in charge here?

It was 10.15 am as Melissa, the school media librarian, called the 10.00 am meeting to start. She had been given responsibility by the principal to lead the teachers and other specialists in a taskforce to determine professional development efforts at their small public high school over the next three years. As she started the meeting, five of the seven team members were present. She quickly moved into discussing the purpose of the committee. After finishing, the other two members arrived. Not wanting them to feel left out, she took the time to go over the committee's purpose yet again. It was now 10.30 am.

Over the course of the next hour, Melissa led them in a brainstorming exercise. She emphasized the need for all ideas to be put forward at this time, no matter how impractical. Unfortunately, a couple of the teachers seemed to dominate, giving almost all of the suggestions. At one point one of the teachers who had not yet spoken offered an idea, which was then immediately criticized and deemed impractical by another member of the group. As the meeting was approaching the end, one of the teachers got up and excused herself, saying that she had some things she needed to get ready before her next class started. In wrapping up at 11.45 am, 15 minutes past the time she had indicated the meeting would end based on the agenda that she had sent out, Melissa thanked everyone for coming and said she hoped they could begin narrowing down the ideas and developing some sense of direction in their next meeting.

- What seemed to go well with this meeting?
- What went poorly in this meeting?
- How could Melissa make the next meeting as productive as possible?

Project ideas

- Explore the culture of a given library but, this time, focus exclusively on issues related to communication by asking only questions about how staff communicate with each other, how staff communicate with the supervisor or supervisors, how the head of the library communicates with external individuals or groups, how the library as an institution gets its message across through its website or any blogs, wikis, social networking sites, etc.
- Explore and critique the blog of your library or a library near you. What's good? What's bad? What's missing?
- Make your own good meeting checklist.

6

Decision-making and leadership

In some senses, this chapter ties together all of the concepts discussed in this book. It also takes us to the last and final step in our journey, making decisions and providing leadership. We make decisions on a daily basis, in both our personal and our professional lives. Some of these decisions are minor and some are of great consequence. So, how do we go about making decisions, and what kinds of biases or misperceptions can throw us off? We will consider a few of these. While many potential models exist, we will explore a few to assist us with our decision-making, especially as it relates to serving in a library management context. We will also explore assessment, as it ties in to both decision-making and leadership. Finally, we will address leadership itself and what it means in a library context. As we do so, and in wrapping up, we will explore some thoughts and ideas found in the prolific area of leadership literature and research.

Some pitfalls and biases in decision-making

Our minds can play tricks on us, and that's a fact. There are a number of ways that our decisions are affected by unconscious factors. According to Richard Thaler and Cass Sunstein (2008), this is due to the fact that while our brains possess a reflective system for responding to stimuli, they also possess an automatic system. Often, we respond using the latter since it kicks in first. This has both obvious and subtle implications, and we shall explore a few of the consequences below.

Anchoring

Anchoring is a subtle but powerful way by which individuals attach themselves to a choice or value without, in many cases, even being conscious that this is what they are doing. For example, Thaler and Sunstein (ibid.) demonstrate this by a simple method. If one were to give someone the figure for the population of Chicago, IL, and then ask them to guess the population of Milwaukee, WI, their estimate will be much higher than if they were to be asked the population of Milwaukee, WI, after being told the population of the much smaller city of Green Bay, WI. Similar results have been obtained by asking people in one group whether or not the Mississippi River is more or less than 500 miles long and asking another group if it is more or less than 5,000 miles, and then following this up by asking how long it actually is. Those given the first choice of higher or lower than 500 miles versus 5,000 miles tend to make much lower estimates (Annenberg/CPB, 1989). A similar experiment had researchers ask participants to write down the first three digits of their phone number and then write down the date when Genghis Khan died. Despite the fact that there is absolutely no relationship, the three phone number digits affected the estimate that people gave (Hallinan, 2009). The warning here is simple. Be careful not to be anchored by something else prior to making a decision. Research clearly shows that this is easier said than done.

Availability bias/heuristic

The availability bias is both fairly common and straightforward. According to Thaler and Sunstein (2008: 25), people 'assess the likelihood of risks by asking how readily examples come to mind'. Thus people are more afraid of terrorist attacks than sunbathing, or assume that homicides are more common than suicides, when, in fact, sunbathing poses greater danger to more people and suicide is more common. A similar argument has been made when comparing people's perceptions regarding the danger of being killed in either a terrorist attack or a deadly car accident when visiting the Middle East. Most fear the former, when the latter is a much more prevalent danger (Annenberg/CPB, 1989). According to Thaler and Sunstein (2008: 25), 'Biased assessments of risk can perversely influence how we prepare for and respond to crises, business choices, and the political process.' In a work situation such as a library, we may have a tendency to worry about the wrong things. We cannot completely guard against this, but by relying heavily on facts and getting multiple perspectives, it might be possible to avoid mistakes of this kind.

Representative bias

When it comes to representative bias, our minds are truly playing tricks on us. One of the most famous cases involves giving participants details about an individual's background and then asking them to make an inference about the individual. For example, participants are first told: 'Linda is 31 years old, single, outspoken and very bright. She majored in philosophy. As a student, she was deeply concerned with issues of discrimination and social justice and also participated in anti-nuclear demonstrations.' They are then asked if she is more likely to be a 'bank teller' or a 'bank teller and active in the feminist movement'. Even though the former category is logically more inclusive and thus the better choice, most people, affected by the bit of history which precedes it, select the latter (Mellers et al., 2001: 269).

Framing

While a couple of specific positive philosophies relative to the concept of framing will be listed below, it should be noted that framing a problem or decision has a powerful impact on the subsequent actions taken. The most powerful aspect of how issues can be framed relates to gains and losses. If a question is framed in terms of a loss, people will be hesitant to select a given choice, whereas if it is framed as a gain the opposite is true. For example, if one were very ill and was told that a treatment had a 10 per cent death rate after five years, people will be less likely to opt for the treatment than if they were told that there is a 90 per cent survival rate after five years (Thaler and Sunstein, 2008).

Too many choices

According to Thaler and Sunstein (ibid.: 97), 'Social science research reveals that as the choices become more numerous and/or vary on more dimensions, people are more likely to adopt simplifying strategies.' These simplifying strategies can lead to both common mistakes and predictive behavior. Thaler and Sunstein's book, *Nudge: Improving Decisions about Health, Wealth, and Happiness*, offers profound insights into what they refer to as choice architecture. Essentially, we can be nudged to make better decisions if the choices are presented in certain ways. More specifically, we should create default choices that are the better options for individuals. This relates to everything from placing fruit at eye level on the children's lunch counter at school as opposed to, say, junk food to having retirement programs that default towards a certain percentage of one's pay and an appropriate diversity of funds. A brief mention of their work may be supplemented by research reported in Dan Ariely's equally masterful book entitled *Predictably Irrational: The Hidden Forces that Shape Our Decisions*. Ariely (2008) adds to this aspect of choice architecture by pointing out that too many choices can lead to paralysis in making any choice. In one study, for example, some customers at a grocery store were given a multitude of special jams to sample while others were given only a few. The customers exposed to fewer samples bought more jam. The others, one may suspect, suffered from jam overload. In a practical application, it might in some cases be better as a library manager to present a limited number of choices or options to one's staff rather than providing too many choices and creating confusion and paralysis.

Some models for making decisions

We can all benefit from solving problems and making decisions in a more purposeful way. As stated above, many biases and distortions can creep their way into our decision-making processes. Numerous models exist for taking a more concerted approach, and it is worth examining a few to see how they might apply to the work of a library manager. I have come to believe that the value in these is not that they provide any specific formulaic approach that needs to be rigidly followed. Rather, they can improve our thinking, help us to avoid the blind spots mentioned earlier and also force us, at times, out of our comfort zone, hopefully to help us reach a better decision with regard to a given problem or situation. According to Judith Gordon (2002), the most basic approach to decision-making is to analyze a given problem, move into setting objectives, seek alternatives, evaluate the different alternatives to choose which one would work best, implement the decision and then evaluate the results. While this rational approach applies very readily, more specific and detailed approaches to problem-solving and decision-making are discussed below.

The four frames

One very popular approach applied to decision-making is Bolman and Deal's four frames. This has been utilized by both experienced professionals, such as those who participate in the annual ACRL/Harvard Leadership Institute course, and library science students working on group-based case study projects (Moniz, 2009). In their book *Reframing Organizations: Artistry, Choice, and Leadership*, Bolman and Deal (2008) lay out a case for their frames and describe how to apply them to solving problems and making decisions. The four frames are the structural, human resource, political and symbolic.

The structural frame refers primarily to organizational architecture. There is at least some implied connection to culture as well, but the emphasis is more upon formal reporting lines, policies, procedures, etc. Of the four frames, it is the most rational. It denotes an emphasis upon effectiveness, but especially as it relates to efficiency. In a library, for example, if one were to consider a problem from the structural frame, one might ask questions about cross-training, leadership structure, project management, etc. To carry this example further into the realm of the concrete, in a small academic library with only a handful of librarians, considerable cross-training may be necessary. In a larger academic library this may not be the case. In terms of leadership structure, generally speaking, a smaller organization should be flatter (ibid.).

How, then, does thinking from the structural frame affect and enhance decision-making? While the structural frame is fairly easy to explain, its application is always context specific. That is, one needs to consider a unique set of variables and a particular problem in order to see how it may be of use. Libraries, just like many workplaces, suffer from a multitude of challenges. Say, for example, one project or challenge that the library staff faced was a need to redesign the library website. From a structural perspective, the most important question to ask might be how to structure and empower a group of librarians to get this done. In doing so, concerns such as balancing representation across the library and including those with the necessary experience and skills would be involved. There would also be a need to establish other structural elements such as goals, timetables, etc.

Before exploring the other frames it is worth providing an additional problem-based example of how the structural frame might be applied. Suppose, for example, library meetings were dominated by someone other than the designated leader of the group, and as a result the voices of others in the group were not heard. In our example, let's pretend the library director is running the meeting. From a structural problem-solving perspective, the dilemma could be viewed as a failure on the part of the director to assert his or her structural authority. Thus a targeted effort on his or her part in this regard could go a long way towards improving the meetings.

The human resource perspective differs considerably from the structural. As opposed to a focus on structures, policies and procedures, the human resource frame leads one to pay attention to the people in the organization. This approach tends to focus on hiring the right people, motivating and empowering employees and retaining staff. Much has already been said about interpersonal skills and their importance to any competent manager. In this frame, these skills are paramount. As with the structural frame, it is necessary to apply a couple of randomly selected contexts to illustrate best how this approach fits (ibid.).

Let's consider, once again, a library that needs to redesign its website. From the structural perspective, we would have asked critical questions about the skills, representation, timeline, etc., necessary. From the human resource perspective, we might begin to consider other factors by asking additional key questions. Is there a person on the staff who has a special interest or desire to be involved in this project and thus might be a good person to help move it along? How much room should be made to solicit feedback from the library staff as a whole in order to ensure buy-in to the final product? How do people feel about the website as it is and in terms of what it could be? By exploring the project from questions framed from the human resource view, another critical dimension to decision-making and problem-solving is thus considered. Take, as well, the human resource perspective on the meeting that has been dominated by someone other than the library director. This also brings up some important questions to consider. How does this make everyone in the meeting feel? Does the fact that one person dominates and the leader does not balance the meeting affect the motivation of staff to follow through on decisions made in this context? The frames don't necessarily ever provide a specific answer. That said, they can shed an interesting light on problems that can, in turn, help us to find appropriate solutions.

Yet another frame that Bolman and Deal discuss is the symbolic. This one is a little bit more unusual than those mentioned so far. We are fairly conscious about our personal interactions on a daily basis and can usually explain the structures applicable in an organization that we have been a part of for a long time. We do not, however, tend to dwell much upon the symbolic perspective on a day-to-day basis. When we consider the symbolic, we might equate it to theatre both literally and figuratively. In my class, I typically begin our discussion on this point by showing a couple of video clips. One of my favorites is a scene from *Casablanca*. In it, Nazi officers are sitting in a bar when they begin singing the 'Das Deutschlandlied' (the German national anthem). Victor Laszlo (played by Paul Henreid), one of the French resistance leaders, is incensed, and gets the band to start playing 'La Marseillaise' (the French national anthem). The crowd quickly joins in and drowns out the Germans (Curtiz, 1943). One could hardly demonstrate expert use of the symbolic frame any better. No words could match the emotions evinced by the singing of the anthem in terms of instilling hope into the crowd. Examples of lighter note are readily accessible in sports. For example, after a particularly bad loss in a season that would ultimately lead to a Super Bowl victory, the head coach of the New England Patriots actually dug a hole and buried the game ball in front of the team, telling them that they would be leaving that game behind and moving forward. In more pedestrian circumstances, one is not always fighting the Nazis or getting paid millions of dollars to play in the National Football League. Still, the library profession does have some lofty ideals which it stands for, including free access to information and the need to take a stand against censorship. Managers and leaders need to consider the organizational values that they wish to convey as well. In considering this perspective, emotional appeals through the use of powerful symbols, props and staging are key (Bolman and Deal, 2008).

Taking the symbolic frame and exploring it alongside the structural and human resource frames, we can see how it may apply yet another layer to our thinking and decision-making processes. In redesigning the library website, we have already considered issues such as the structure of the workgroup and the feelings and motivations of staff. What we have not yet considered is the symbolic importance of the website itself. As discussed in the previous chapter, not only what is written on a website but also how it is designed has important implications. One might very well consider the overall symbolic impact that is intended by the site. To give just a small example of symbolism in this regard, consider the Seattle Public Library's homepage (www.spl.lib.wa.us). When going to this page, one is welcomed not just by a greeting in English but also in another language as well (in three successive refreshes to my web browser I was welcomed in Somali, Tigrina and Vietnamese). It's a simple touch, but it makes a fairly powerful symbolic statement about the importance of diversity to the Seattle Public Library. In a broader sense, the symbolic frame goes back to our discussion of what managers and leaders actually do as well. Staff will look at their behavior rather closely. An otherwise busy library director engaged in an important task who drops everything to assist a patron sends a powerful symbolic message as to what really matters.

The fourth and final frame to be considered is the political. As in our discussion of bureaucracy in the first chapter, many librarians automatically associate the word 'political' with negative behaviors and circumstances. Viewing problems from the political perspective, however, can serve to remind managers of critical elements that affect their role. Organizations usually consist of a variety of overlapping coalitions. Power and the ability to make decisions are important. And conflict is normal. These factors, in turn, lead an effective manager to take certain actions. For example, he or she should recognize the power of setting an agenda (both in terms of daily work schedules and projects and in terms of meetings, etc.), the need to map the political arena to determine who the important people are for the library and its staff to have support from in order to meet goals, the need to network and build relationships that positively impact on the library and its staff, and the need to make ethical choices that help maintain the long-term integrity of both the manager and the library (ibid.).

In our web redesign example, it may be important to consider the views of politically important constituencies. For example, a public library manager might consider the opinions of local elected officials or how the website might be used to provide useful information to the community relative to an important city planning project. In an academic library, important constituencies might include how the library website might relate to other departmental websites. In terms of the meeting run amuck, political considerations would include the relative power that has been given to the person hijacking the meeting.

Six thinking hats

A similar approach to that taken by Bolman and Deal has been suggested by Edward de Bono, author of *Six Thinking Hats*. De Bono's hats essentially work like frames. 'The white hat is concerned with facts and figures... The red hat gives the emotional view... The black hat is cautious and careful... The yellow hat is optimistic and covers hope and positive thinking... The green hat indicates creativity and new ideas... The blue hat is concerned with control, the organization of the thinking process, and the other hats' (de Bono, 1999: 13–15). Given our website redesign as a context, the white hat approach would consider facts such as what information needs to go on the site, what information is currently on the site, etc. The red hat approach would be similar to the human resource frame in considering people's feelings and emotions relative to the site. The black hat approach would remind the group charged with redesign not to throw the baby out with the bathwater by considering what elements in the current design might be maintained. The yellow hat approach might help serve as a reminder to the group that it will be a long process and of the need for celebrating small successes along the way. The green hat approach would encourage brainstorming and outside-the-box thinking. Lastly, the blue hat approach would consider the process by which the website redesign would take place and the role of team members in the process.

One of the differences between Bolman and Deal and de Bono is that Bolman and Deal suggest individuals themselves apply more than one frame to a given situation. De Bono suggests, however, using the hats by assigning different people to each. In other words, somebody might be asked to 'wear the black hat' and thus encourage a conservative approach among the group or, conversely, to 'wear the green hat' and continually force the group towards considering unconventional alternatives to a given problem.

The decision-making tree

One last approach to making decisions which will be discussed here is the decision-making tree. The decision-making tree or normative decision model is a contingency model which grew out of the work of Fred Fiedler (1964), whose work was discussed in the first chapter. Building on Fiedler's point that decisions are made within specific contexts, Vroom and Jago (2007) set out to create a systematic way to approach decision-making and problem-solving. Two initial factors that they considered of great importance were the quality of a decision and the need for acceptance. That is, certain decisions have a greater impact than others and some decisions require greater buy-in from staff in order for them to be effective. On their next set of dimensions, they considered various styles that could be applied to making a given decision. These ranged from solving the problem entirely on one's own, gathering information from others (although not necessarily telling them what for) and then making the decision, consulting with appropriate group members individually and then making a decision, sharing a problem with the group for a discussion but then making the final decision, and finally, offering a problem up for discussion and having the group decide on a course of action. It is worth noting that, by combining these two dimensions, this model suggests using a tree where one simply moves along the branches to find out which approach is best for a given decision (Dubrin, 1998). While the process is very straightforward, not all situations lend themselves to being perfectly characterized. Thus I would suggest using this concept more as a way of thinking.

Before moving on, let's consider how this model might apply in a library. Let's pretend that you are considering a policy change in the library that will be a major benefit to patrons but will require all of the staff to carry it out effectively, relatively unsupervised. You can see right away where the library director would need the staff to buy in to such a decision. Thus, making it a group decision or at least allowing the group to have input before making a final decision would be of value. One qualification or caveat needs to be stated, however, when considering opening up an important decision of this nature to the group. Research has indicated that most experienced managers are hesitant to have a wide-open discussion on an issue that they know will bring up *overwhelming* conflict among staff (Vroom and Jago, 2007). Likewise, an important decision affecting patrons but *not* requiring staff buy-in might be made by the director on his or her own or after one-on-one consultation with appropriate staff. Interestingly, in issues of lesser importance this process can be even further simplified. Decisions of low importance or quality, according to this model, which do not need a commitment from the library staff can also just be made by the director. Not everything needs to be put to a vote, even in a library with a highly participatory culture. Of course, issues of lesser importance that would probably not raise a negative degree of conflict and need staff commitment can just as easily be put to the group if there is time to do so.

Assessments

Before moving on to our discussion of leadership, it is important to note that when making decisions as discussed above, assessment of current services and processes plays a critical role. Assessment provides a library manager and a library's staff with the kind of information to inform better both the day-to-day decision-making needs of a manager and the long-term planning associated with leadership.

LibQUAL+

LibQUAL+ is a widely used tool in academic libraries that seeks to measure service quality through the administration of a standardized series of survey questions posed to library users. It originated out of the work done by Parasuraman et al. (1985) at Texas A&M University more than 20 years ago. Originally targeted for use in the for-profit sector, this tool sought to measure the gaps between customer perceptions of service, their expectations for minimally acceptable service and their desires for optimum service levels. Along with other indicators, one key measure that is determined is referred to as the 'zone of tolerance', which is derived by measuring the difference between minimum and desired scores. Another indicator is the 'service adequacy gap', which is derived by calculating the difference between the minimum and perceived performance. Lastly, the 'service superiority gap' derives from the difference between perceived and desired performance. After several years of tweaking, the survey now consists of 22 items and a comment box. Due to some testing of instrumentation and methodology led by Thompson, the Likert scale employed has been expanded to include nine levels from which a participant may select. Furthermore, the survey is administered through a web-based instrument. The typical procedure involves the random selection of institutional e-mail addresses. Users are then sent an initial e-mail (along with a follow-up e-mail at a later date) asking them to fill out the survey (Thompson et al., 2001; Snyder, 2002). The major drawbacks are that, since it needs to apply to all types of academic libraries, the questions may not be best for your specific institutional concerns, and it costs more than $2,000 to participate.

Annual surveys

Many libraries have an annual survey that is done online. The availability of inexpensive, or even free, online tools such as those found at www.zoomerang.com and www.surveymonkey.com has allowed more and more libraries to be able to gather data from users on a regular and efficient basis. In an academic library, a link to such a survey can easily be sent out to students and faculty alike. In a public library, both users and non-users in the community could be surveyed by gathering or creating appropriate e-mail lists. The value of this approach to gathering data is the fact that such instruments can be readily tailored to questions of specific interest, as opposed to being confined to questions associated with a nationally normed test such as LibQUAL+.

Best/worst or strength/weaknesses/ opportunities/threats

Best/worst or strengths/weaknesses/opportunities/threats (SWOTs) types of analyses can be very useful, especially in gathering data from library staff. In the case of a best/worst exercise, one would ask staff to brainstorm individually about the best aspects of the library. They then share those bests with the group. Following this, the group would be asked to provide their own individual rankings from the list. Likewise, this would also be done with the 'worsts' associated with the library. The facilitator would then compile a report useful for decision-making and planning.

SWOTs have been used for a number of years in business situations. They work similar to the best/worst exercise. In this case, however, staff are asked to identify strengths, weaknesses, opportunities and threats facing the library and then to rank them accordingly.

Focus groups

One other approach worth mentioning here in gathering data to be utilized in decision-making and leadership is focus groups. Again, focus groups have been used for a long time in the business world to test new products. In libraries they can be used to follow up on survey data and/or to probe further into areas of concern. For example, a survey might note that students are unhappy about library hours. Probing in a focus group might reveal that the problem is actually very specific times when access is needed. It could also, in this case, reveal an issue whereby students are unaware of virtual resources accessible to them even when the physical library is closed.

Leadership

Having a certain approach to making decisions, avoiding various pitfalls and having good data to back one up are all necessary precursors to good leadership. According to one source, there are more than 30,000 publications (books, articles, etc.) in existence regarding the topic of leadership (Dubrin, 1998). There are almost as many definitions for leadership. Many seek to establish its definition by contrasting it with management. In the words of John Kotter (1996: 25):

> Management is a set of processes that can keep a complicated system of people and technology running smoothly... Leadership is a set of processes that creates organizations in the first place or adapts them to significantly changing circumstances. Leadership defines what the future should look like, aligns people with that vision, and inspires them to make it happen despite the obstacles.

Likewise, Warren Bennis and Burt Nanus (1997: 39) describe the difference between managers and leaders as 'the difference between routine problem solvers and problem finders'. While these are apt descriptions, I prefer that of James Kouzes and Barry Posner (1995: 31), who state, 'To get a feel for the true essence of leadership, assume that everyone who works with you is a volunteer.'

Some of the earliest scholarship on leadership focused on what is commonly referred to as trait theory. This theory essentially posited that leaders exhibit certain key qualities. One premise of this theory, since discredited, is that leaders are somehow born and not made. Rather, a new emphasis can be found on the *development* of certain traits and characteristics (Gordon, 2002). In exploring the characteristics of great leaders, from both profit and non-profit realms, extensive research has shown that the four most important qualities are honesty, the ability to be forward-looking, the ability to inspire others and general competency (Kouzes and Posner, 1995). As stated in the previous chapter, leaders are also typically great communicators. In the words of Bennis and Nanus (1997: 37), 'Leaders articulate and define what has previously remained implicit and unsaid; then they invent images, metaphors, and models that provide a focus for new attention.' Likewise, Kouzes and Posner (1995: 134) state, 'Successful leaders use metaphors and figures of speech; they give examples, tell stories, and relate anecdotes; they draw word pictures; and they offer quotations and recite slogans.' One can see here a clear association with the symbolic frame previously discussed. And, of course, as stated in the previous chapter, the listening part of communicating is equally as important as what leaders say.

Communicating, and more specifically the relationships that we establish and build upon, is the most important asset of a leader. In the words of Kouzes and Posner (ibid.: 151), 'In the more than 550 original cases that we studied, we didn't encounter a single example of extraordinary achievement that occurred without the active involvement and support of many people. And this hasn't changed with our subsequent research.' This is accomplished in a number of ways. As mentioned above, honesty is the most important expectation we have of leaders. Closely associated with this is trust. The active support of others cannot be achieved without trust. And, as most of us are taught from an early age and through experience, trust needs to be earned, especially if we want library staff to engage in challenging endeavors. According to Kouzes and Posner (ibid.: 29), 'We're willing to forgive a few minor transgressions, a slip of the tongue, a misspoken word, a careless act. But there comes a time when enough is enough. And when leaders have used up all of their credibility, it's nearly impossible to get it back.' Robert Sutton, a Stanford University professor and author of *The No Asshole Rule*, would frame it a bit differently. In extreme circumstances, he would say that there is a difference between a temporary asshole (which we can all be) and a certified asshole (reserved for a special few). While we won't dwell here on negative leadership, the utterly devastating impact of bullies in leadership positions which Sutton (2007) describes in detail cannot be overstated. Studies have shown that they can do tremendous damage not just to those bullied, but even to those who witness the bullying. It is okay to make a mistake when dealing with others. It is not okay not to apologize, not to learn from the mistake, or to make it a pattern of behavior. Furthermore, as Covey (1989) would say, there is no trick or gimmick to get people to trust your leadership. It usually starts with a genuine desire to get to know better, understand and support others, largely facilitated through high-quality communication. The relationship between organizational culture, as discussed earlier, and the qualities of a leader could not be clearer. 'When contributors' thoughts and ideas are shot down or ridiculed, the climate isn't safe; neither is it conducive to vulnerability (the precursor to opening up and placing trust in another person)' (Kouzes and Posner, 1995: 177). Thus we need to listen carefully, and communicate with sensitivity and respect.

Through their ability to listen and respond to others, earn their trust and communicate through a variety of means, leaders become more effective. Leaders must also be experts at empowerment. Kouzes and Posner (ibid.: 185–7) state that '*we become the most powerful when we give our own power away*... the more people believe that they can influence and control the organization, the greater organizational effectiveness and member satisfaction will be'. They go on to note that great leaders whom they studied 'knew that power isn't a zero-sum commodity, requiring that for others to have more, the leader must have less'.

In my view, all these factors come together to create a high-performing organization or library. Leaders who have trust will get the best from their staff and, in turn, will be able to articulate a more prescient and higher-quality vision. Thus there are some very practical concerns here on the part of the leader. According to Bennis and Nanus (1997: 89), in their discussion of images and vision, 'In all these cases, the leader may have been the one who chose the image from those available at the moment, articulated it, gave it form and legitimacy, and focused attention on it, but the leader was only rarely the one who conceived of the vision in the first place.' Libraries have been affected by so many external elements since the birth of electronic resources and other recent changes in our society that a more apt statement could not be made. One approach to leadership suggests that a leader should surround himself or herself with others who excel where he or she is weak. This is good advice. Still, in the library world it appears that change is so widespread and constant that this applies more widely as well. I remember being swamped with other tasks as staff members at my campus and others brought blogs, wikis, social networking, LibGuides, Second Life, etc., to my attention when they came along. There was simply no way for me to have the time to investigate all of these on my own. Yet awareness of them and how they might apply to or impact on the future of our library was critical. Likewise, for example, our information literacy program is very well designed and planned out, thanks to the work of successive instruction librarians who have had the talent and drive to create and develop it. I could easily refer as well to the design of our technical services efforts, which were developed by another staff member showing great individual initiative. Staff simply must be given the authority to explore and try new things. One last related note on this point comes from Kouzes and Posner (1995: 199), 'Leaders who want to strengthen their constituents ensure that they're highly visible and that individual and group efforts get noticed and recognized.' You simply cannot do too much of this. You must both empower employees and be sure they receive proper recognition for their efforts. While this latter part deals with the topic of motivation, in the context of leadership it means something more as well: one is concerned less about immediate motivational issues and more about the long-term growth of individual staff in terms of both self-confidence and actual ability.

Yet another important thing is to lead by example. Again, we go back to the issue of impacting on culture and connecting it to high-quality leadership. At its most basic level, a leader should not ask another person to do work that they would not do or have not done themselves. This aspect of leadership relates very closely to teaching. We must both pay our own dues and model behavior. Of course, this is probably the most difficult aspect of leadership since it denotes a daily struggle. Daniel Goleman's concept of emotional intelligence and Stephen Covey's seven habits were discussed at length earlier. These deal almost entirely with managing oneself and maintaining self-control at all times. When interactions with others occur daily, a leader must be vigilant. He or she will slip at times, but must continue to address shortcomings in this regard.

In studying leaders, many authors have connected them explicitly to change. This seems entirely appropriate. In their comprehensive studies on leadership, Kouzes and Posner (ibid.: 9) relate how most leaders talk about leadership. They often have a premier experience that has helped frame their thinking. This could have been anything from developing a new product or service to 'the start-up of a new plant or business'. They go on to state, 'Not one person claimed to have done his or her personal best by keeping things the same. *In short, all leaders challenge the process.*' For this reason, it is worth closing by briefly exploring John Kotter and his unique approach to leading change.

Leading change

John Kotter, a recognized expert on leadership, has outlined an eight-step approach to leading change in organizations. His work readily applies to non-profits and libraries. While Kotter would insist that his eight steps should be followed to some degree as a formula, I would once again offer up his ideas as general ways to improve thinking and, in this case, leading.

The first of Kotter's steps is to create a sense of urgency. In his words, 'Never underestimate the magnitude of the forces that reinforce complacency and that help maintain the status quo' (Kotter, 1996: 42). For one last time, it might be worth revisiting the economic collapse of recent days. In hindsight, it seems that some of the best and brightest financial minds became entirely too complacent about everything from what they believed was the guaranteed rise of value in the housing market to the integrity and rising value of the US stock market in general. Libraries too can be complacent. A good leader must force himself or herself and his or her staff to question assumptions and not rest on past success.

The second of Kotter's steps, while dealing a bit more directly with larger organizations, focuses on creating strong teams and coalitions (ibid.). We could go back yet again to our website redesign to consider what expertise, position, power, personality mixes, etc., might be needed to guide the team on this point. The idea of building trust also applies, not just between leader and followers, but among group members as well.

Kotter's third step is to create a powerful vision. We've already covered this need as well, but he makes an additional point worth mentioning here in his discussion of considering various constituencies. 'A good vision can demand sacrifices from some or all of these groups in order to produce a better future, but it never ignores the long-term interests of anyone. Visions that try to help some constituencies by trampling on the rights of others tend to be associated with the most nefarious demigods' (ibid.: 73). One role of an academic library director, for example, is to balance the needs of students, faculty and staff. For example, staff may not want to meet reasonable demands of students and a nudge might be required as a result. Likewise, a director might balance a request by students for the library to be open 24/7 not only with usage statistics and budget considerations, but also with the legitimate morale issues for a staff member having to work from, say, midnight until 8.00 am.

The fourth of Kotter's steps involves communicating a vision. Again, he makes a point that relates very directly to the library environment: 'all widespread communication in a change effort must be jargon free' (ibid.: 91). How often, as librarians, do we speak of OPACs, Boolean searching, nesting search terms, peer-reviewed journals, etc., without adequately explaining what we are talking about? Likewise, our vision for the library might also be full of jargon or our own perspective. It needs to be translated into language that others will understand.

The fifth step focuses on empowerment (ibid.). We've already talked about the importance of this, but it is worth relating here the other side of empowerment; that is, the need to remove barriers. I have often seen within my role as library director the need to remove impediments when a highly energized staff member is trying to accomplish something but running into a bureaucratic quagmire.

Kotter's sixth step relays the need to create short-term wins (ibid.). This is an important step that can't be overestimated. In our library, we periodically engage in planning. Our strategic plan provides an overarching framework for accomplishing our mission. We have discussed and reviewed this strategic plan as a group. That said, we also use the strategic plan to develop annual goals. These are specific targets that we can aim at. By having annual goals, we are able to celebrate short-term successes as we move towards fulfilling our mission. This keeps us focused and motivated. Since this book is intended to be practical, a sample of an annual plan is included as an appendix.

Kotter's seventh and eighth steps, which focus on consolidating changes and anchoring them in the culture, serve as a warning (ibid.). Changes can easily be undermined in the long run. In some cases, structural changes may be necessary to solidify changes. This point also serves to connect us back up with the socialization process as well. If major changes are truly sought, it may be necessary to change the screening process for new employees. We tend to seek others who would be a good fit for our organization. One should question, however, whether a candidate is a good fit for where the organization was or where it is going.

Final thoughts on leadership

A couple of last points need to be iterated before concluding our exploration of leadership: the need for mistakes and the equally important need to learn from them in general. In describing great leaders, Bennis and Nanus (1997: 67) state, 'Almost every "false step" was regarded as an opportunity... They were convinced that they could learn...' Leaders must accept that both they and others will make mistakes. It is how you handle them that is more important.

Kouzes and Posner (1995: 334–5) state, 'Knowledge and skill, like other assets, depreciate in value if left unattended... Learning – including knowing how to and realizing the importance of – is the sine qua non for both personal and organizational vitality.' Likewise, Bennis and Nanus (1997: 176) state, 'Leaders are perpetual learners. Some are voracious readers... Many learn from other people... Learning is the essential fuel for the leader, the source of high-octane energy that keeps up the momentum by continually sparking new understanding, new ideas and challenges.' If this is true for other organizations, it is doubly true for libraries. In my opinion, if there are two things that a library manager should be known for, it should be for both focusing and targeting his or her own learning and for fostering and supporting learning and growth opportunities among staff. And I can think of no better way to end our topic and this book than by encouraging you to explore more, broaden your horizons and learn from the experiences that lie ahead.

Thoughts for consideration or discussion

- Which of the four frames do you think you'd be naturally inclined to use the most and why?
- Which of the six thinking hats do you think you'd be naturally inclined to use and why?
- What are your greatest leadership strengths and weaknesses?
- Who are your three favorite leaders and why?
- What kinds of assessments are used to assist in the planning process at your library or a library near you?

Case study: the Winslow Homer Institute for Art

Mark had been a successful reference librarian for several years. He also had a prior background in the business world as the manager of a small retail establishment. Knowing of his reputation as a diligent worker and a competent librarian, the president of a newly established small college, the Winslow Homer Institute for Art, approached Mark and asked him to serve as the institution's first library director. Mark was given the following information.

- The school would open in six months, with the library occupying a space of 12,000 square feet on the ground floor of the main building (already under construction). Mark would have some input in the set-up of the facility and more so when it came to furniture and equipment.
- The school would have an initial enrollment of approximately 600 students, but would grow over a period of five years to as many as 1,500 students.

- All students would be in an art-related program, although these programs would vary within the field quite a bit. A catalog explaining the various program and course options was currently at the printers.

- Students would be studying towards bachelor's degrees and so would need to take academic courses as well.

- Most faculty would be selected and hired along with other staff at least three months before the first students started classes.

- In addition to the library director, the library would have one full-time and one part-time librarian in its first year of operation. In its second year an additional full-time librarian would be hired, and in its third year an additional part-time librarian would be hired. The library would also be allowed to hire several student assistants.

- The library director would be given complete discretion in spending $300,000 of initial collection development funds, which could be applied to books, databases, periodicals, etc. This figure would go down to $125,000 for successive budget years.

- The library director would have complete discretion in the organization of the library and its materials, including the selection of an online cataloging system.

- The library director would be given wide latitude in establishing the focus and mission of the library in conjunction with that of the larger organization, which would be 'To foster and support premier educational programs in art-related fields that allow graduates to pursue successful and rewarding careers.'

After meeting with the president and receiving this information, Mark decides to take the job.

- What are the issues that Mark faces? Can they be prioritized?

- How should Mark address each issue in turn (e.g. hiring staff, doing collection development, setting policies, etc.)?

- Is there enough time to do everything that needs to be done or do some issues need to be shelved for later?

- How will Mark lead the library? What will the culture be like?

- Does he have all the information that he needs? What kinds of questions does he need to ask?

Project ideas

- Interview an experienced library manager. Ask them about their greatest challenges and how they handle them. Ask them how they communicate with staff and make decisions.

- Interview a librarian or library manager about a significant problem they faced in the workplace. On your own or with a group, analyze the problem using Bolman and Deal's four frames or de Bono's six hats. After analyzing and discussing, consider how you would solve the problem.

- Keeping to one page, write down your philosophy on what good leadership is and is not. Have others you work with or attend class with do the same. Share and discuss your philosophies.

Appendix: sample of a basic annual plan

Priority 1

Manage staff turnover by hiring appropriate replacements with competitive wages.

Timeline

- Post position for open part-time role in August 2008.
- Interview and select candidate to fill open part-time position by 2 September.
- Rank remaining candidates and hold for other potential part-time position opening later in the year.
- Post full-time position opening by 15 September.
- Begin interviews immediately with departure of the current instruction librarian (anticipated in November 2008).
- Hire for full-time position.

Success indicators

- New part-time position is in place for the start of school.
- Transition to the new full-time person (and possibly new part-time person) occurs with minimal disruption to information literacy programs (all modules are taught as planned as well as critical specialized instruction session).

Results

Positions were posted and interviews conducted. This led to not just the hiring of a new part-time person but identifying a larger role for the previous 12-hours per week part-time person. While there was great concern about replacing the full-time instruction librarian, this was done effectively as well. The transition has been smooth and all staff deserve credit for the professionalism and support provided throughout the transition.

Priority 2

Continuing to support and develop our highly successful information literacy program through the use of our new audience response system technology.

Timeline

- Develop new lesson plans for pilot class that will use the new technology in August 2008.
- Meet with the head of information technology and the academic dean before the start of school to determine a plan for purchasing a specifically identified system for library use.
- Secure the new technology and establish policy for its use by the start of school.
- Experiment with the technology further by using it in at least one standardized information literacy session by the spring semester.

Success indicators

- Devices purchased and in place in time for the start of the fall semester.
- Use of the devices in English composition courses for initial standard presentation of information literacy throughout the academic year.
- Feedback collected informally from faculty determining the effectiveness of the technology.

- Experimental implementation of the use of the technology in a science course by the end of the spring semester.

Results

Despite some initial challenges regarding the implementation of a new technology, 40 audience response system devices were purchased for use in library instruction. These devices were ultimately integrated into all information literacy sessions, with positive feedback from faculty and students. A detailed study was also conducted regarding their use in science courses. A benefit of the study was that the plan for instruction in these courses was evaluated and revamped to a considerable degree. Information literacy continues to be integrated on a very broad scale throughout the institution through partnerships between librarians and faculty.

Priority 3

Raise the visibility and respect for librarians as educators on campus by participating regularly in faculty in-services and library-staff-only development efforts.

Timeline

- Librarians will participate in all activities related to faculty orientation and faculty development.

Success indicator

- Attendance at orientation and faculty in-services.

Results

Every faculty in-service including most departmental in-services had attendance by one or more librarians. At least one librarian actually presented at each of the three main in-services as well (i.e. this far exceeds our goal).

Priority 4

Enhance and expand the student experience by piloting expanded book access for students and faculty through the system provided by the newly joined consortium and assess results.

Timeline

- Mailers and other materials necessary will be ordered in August 2008.
- The system will be in place for the start of the fall semester.

Success indicators

- Students and faculty begin using the system at the start of the fall semester.
- The system is evaluated on an ongoing basis with a final evaluation to come at the end of the 2008/2009 academic year.

Results

The loan system was piloted, but sending and retrieving books from a consortium that was too widely dispersed proved too cumbersome, with two-week wait times for materials being normal. To our surprise we also became an extreme net lender. It was determined that the service would be a detriment and not a benefit to our students. As a result the pilot was ended and interlibrary loan services, previously available only to faculty, were extended to students as a replacement.

Priority 5

The library will begin to play an enhanced role in campus teaching and learning as it relates to faculty development, especially with regard to assistance in researching, planning and resource development.

Timeline

- The library director will meet with the director of faculty development at the local research university and the academic dean in the summer of 2008 to discuss faculty development.

- Under the direction of the academic dean, the library director will assist in the planning and implementation of an initial orientation session related to faculty development.
- Under the direction of the academic dean, the library director will assist in further planning and implementation of faculty development efforts.

Success indicator

- The library director will meet the expectations of the academic dean in providing assistance with planning and implementation efforts regarding faculty development.

Results

The library director co-chaired and helped plan all faculty in-services for the 2008/2009 academic year. Other librarians on staff also participated as presenters.

Priority 6

Launch the 2008/2009 academic year with a major 'promotional day' highlighting 'library survival skills'.

Timeline

- Materials will be printed and other necessary items acquired in August 2008.
- Promotional materials announcing the day will be distributed in the first week of school.
- The promotional day will occur in early September.

Success indicator

- The promotional day will occur and will witness at minimum a 100 per cent increase in gate counts for that day.

Results

While 100 per cent increase in gate count was not achieved, this was probably an artificial goal. The promotional materials were created and a day was targeted for launching it. Based on experiences and feedback from students it would appear that promotional activities highlighting the library would do well to extend beyond the library in the future (i.e. outreach, etc.).

Priority 7

Conduct the second year of SAILS assessment sampling to start learning what our students are gaining through our information literacy efforts and initiatives.

Timeline

- Faculty who will assist will be identified prior to the start of school.
- Faculty will be contacted no later than the first week of school and be asked to participate.

Success indicator

- 200 students representing a reasonable cross-section of the student body will be sampled using the SAILS instrument by the end of the fall semester.

Results

The SAILS test was conducted with a reasonable cross-section of students. Test results showed that, in general, students' scores were average. Some initial discussion was on the idea that we would ultimately like our students to be above average on the evaluating resources component.

References

Adams, J.S. (1963) 'Toward an understanding of inequity', *Journal of Abnormal Psychology*, 67(5): 422–36.

Annenberg/CPB (1989) *Judgment and Decision Making; Motivation and Emotion*. South Burlington, VT: Annenberg/CPB.

Anzalone, Filippa M. (2007) 'Servant leadership: a new model for law library leaders', *Law Library Journal*, 99(4): 793–812.

Argyris, Chris (2002) 'Double loop learning, teaching, and research', *Academy of Management Learning and Education*, 1(2): 206–18.

Ariely, Dan (2008) *Predictably Irrational: The Hidden Forces that Shape Our Decisions*. New York: Harper.

Barrett, Deborah J. (2006) 'Strong communication skills a must for today's leaders', *Handbook of Business Strategy*, 7(1): 385–90.

Bassett, Michael (2005) 'Bring new life to meetings', *Association Meetings*, 17(1): 31–3.

Bennis, Warren G. (1961) 'Revisionist theory of leadership', *Harvard Business Review*, 39(1): 27–36, 146–50.

Bennis, Warren G. and Nanus, Burt (1997) *Leaders: Strategies for Taking Charge*. New York: Harper Business.

Berard, Jocelyn (2004) 'Stop the anxiety', *CA Magazine*, 137(10): 27–34.

Bezier, Doug (2007) 'E-mail is dead...', *Fast Company*, 117: 46.

Bolman, Lee G. and Deal, Terrence E. (2008) *Reframing Organizations: Artistry, Choice, and Leadership*. San Francisco, CA: Jossey-Bass.

Buckingham, Marcus and Coffman, Curt (1999) *First Break All the Rules: What the World's Best Managers Do Differently*. New York: Simon & Schuster.

Chan, Donna C. (2006) 'Core competencies and performance management in Canadian public libraries', *Library Management*, 27(3): 144–53.

Chatman, Jennifer A. and Jehn, Karen A. (1994) 'Assessing the relationship between industry characteristics and organizational culture: how different can you be', *Academy of Management Journal*, 37(3): 522–53.

Christensen, John (producer) (2002) *Fish! Catch the Energy, Release the Potential!* Burnsville, MN: ChartHouse International Learning.

Cosier, Richard A. and Dalton, Dan R. (1983) 'Equity theory and time: a reformulation', *Academy of Management Review*, 8(2): 311–19.

Covey, Stephen R. (1989) *Seven Habits of Highly Effective People: Restoring the Character Ethic*. New York: Simon & Schuster.

Covey, Stephen R. (1997) 'Work it out together', *Incentive*, 171(4): 26.

Curtiz, Michael (director) (1943) *Casablanca*. Los Angeles, CA: Warner Brothers.

Dass, Parshotam and Parker, Barbara (1999) 'Strategies for managing human resource diversity: from resistance to learning', *Academy of Management Executive*, 13(2): 68–80.

de Bono, Edward (1999) *Six Thinking Hats*. New York: Little, Brown.

Dubrin, Andrew J. (1998) *Leadership: Research, Findings, Practice, and Skills*. New York: Houghton Mifflin.

Edwards, Mark and Ewen, Ann J. (1996) *360 Feedback: The Powerful New Model for Employee Assessment and Performance Improvement*. New York: American Management Association.

Evans, Carl and Wright, Warren (2008) 'Copy: all users', *Management Services*, 52(1): 24–7.

Fabian, Nelson (1995) 'Communicating effectively – that is the issue', *Journal of Environmental Health*, 58(1): 5.

Fayol, Henri ([1916] 1984) *General and Industrial Management*, translated by Irwin Gray. New York: IEEE.

Fiedler, Fred E. (1964) 'A contingency model of leadership effectiveness', *Advances in Experimental Social Psychology*, 1: 149–90.

Gay, Melvin, Hollandsworth, James G. Jr and Galassi, John P. (1975) 'An assertiveness inventory for adults', *Journal of Counseling Psychology*, 22(4): 340–4.

Goleman, Daniel (1997) *Emotional Intelligence: Why It Can Matter More than IQ*. New York: Bantam Books.

Goleman, Daniel, Boyatzis, Richard and McKee, Annie (2002) *Primal Leadership: Realizing the Power of Emotional Intelligence*. Boston, MA: Harvard Business School Press.

Gordon, Judith R. (2002) *Organizational Behavior: An Organizational Approach*. Upper Saddle River, NJ: Prentice Hall.

Graham, G.H., Unruh, J. and Jennings, P. (1991) 'The impact of nonverbal communication in organizations: a survey of perceptions', *Journal of Business Communication*, 28(1): 45–62.

Greenleaf, Robert K. (1996) *On Becoming a Servant Leader*. San Francisco, CA: Jossey-Bass.

Hallinan, Joseph T. (2009) *Why We Make Mistakes: How We Look Without Seeing, Forget Things in Seconds, and Are All Pretty Sure We Are Way Above Average*. New York: Broadway Books.

Haynes, Marion E. (1997) *Effective Meeting Skills*. Menlo Park, CA: Crisp Learning.

Helms, Ann D. (2008) 'Web posting can cost job, CMS cautions', *Charlotte Observer*, 19 November; available at: *www.charlotte.com* (accessed: 20 June 2009).

Helms, Marilyn M. (ed.) (2000) *Encyclopedia of Management*. Detroit, MI: Thomson Gale.

Hernon, Peter and Rossiter, Nancy (2006) 'Emotional intelligence: which traits are most prized?', *College & Research Libraries*, 67(3): 260–75.

Hernon, Peter, Powell, Ronald R. and Young, Arthur P. (2004) 'Academic library directors: what do they do?', *College & Research Libraries*, 65(6): 538–63.

Herzberg, Frederick I. (1968) 'One more time: how do you motivate employees', *Harvard Business Review*, 46(1): 53–62.

Herzberg, Frederick I. (1974a) 'New perspectives on the will to work', *Management Review*, 63(11): 52–4.

Herzberg, Frederick I. (1974b) 'Motivation-hygiene profiles: pinpointing what ails the organization', *Organizational Dynamics*, 3(2): 18–29.

Herzberg, Frederick I., Mausner, Bernard and Snyderman, Barbara B. ([1959] 1993) *The Motivation to Work*. Edison, NJ: Transaction Publishers.

Hiemstra, Kathleen M. (1999) 'Shake my hand: making the right first impression in business with nonverbal communications', *Business Communications Quarterly*, 62(4): 71–4.

Hopkins, Joel (director) (2009) *Last Chance Harvey*. New York: Overture Films.

Hunter, James C. (2006) *The Servant Leadership Training Course: Achieving Success through Character, Bravery, and Influence*. Louisville, CO: Sounds True.

Jameel, Sabena (2008) 'Making the most of phone consultations', *Pulse*, 68(30): 30–1.

Janda, Louis (2001) *The Psychologist's Book of Personality Tests: 24 Revealing Tests to Identify and Overcome Your Personal Barriers.* New York: John Wiley & Sons.

Katz, Daniel and Kahn, Robert L. (1966) *The Social Psychology of Organizations.* New York: John Wiley & Sons.

Kotter, John P. (1996) *Leading Change.* Boston, MA: Harvard Business School Press.

Kouzes, James M. and Posner, Barry Z. (1995) *The Leadership Challenge: How to Keep Getting Extraordinary Things Done in Organizations.* San Francisco, CA: Jossey-Bass.

Kozel-Gains, Melissa A. and Stoddart, Richard A. (2009) 'Experiments and experiences in liaison activities: lessons from new librarians in integrating technology, face-to-face, and follow-up', *Collection Management*, 34(2): 130–42.

Lencioni, Patrick (2004) *Death By Meeting: A Leadership Fable – About Solving the Most Painful Problem in Business.* San Francisco, CA: Jossey-Bass.

Lewin, Kurt (1947) 'Frontiers in group dynamics: concept, method and reality in social science; social equilibria and social change', *Human Relations*, 1(1): 5–41.

Locke, Edwin A. and Latham, Gary P. (2002) 'Building a practically useful theory of goal setting and task motivation: a 35-year odyssey', *American Psychologist*, 57(9): 705–17.

Locke, Edwin A. and Somers, Richard L. (1987) 'The effects of goal emphasis on performance on a complex task', *Journal of Management Studies*, 24(4): 405–11.

Luthans, Fred (1988) 'Successful versus effective real managers', *Academy of Management Executive*, 2(2): 127–32.

Mancini, John F. (2006) 'E-mail management', *AIIM (Association for Information and Image Management)*, 20(6): 10.

Maslow, Abraham H. (1943) 'A theory of human motivation', *Psychological Review*, 50(4): 370–96.

Maslow, Abraham H. ([1954] 1987) *Motivation and Personality.* New York: Longman.

Mayo, Elton ([1933] 1960) *The Human Problems of an Industrial Civilization.* New York: Viking Press.

McCaskey, Michael B. (1979) 'The hidden messages managers send', *Harvard Business Review*, 57(6): 135–48.

McClelland, David C. (1987) *Human Motivation.* Cambridge: Cambridge University Press.

McClelland, David C. and Burnham, David H. (1977) 'Power is the great motivator', *McKinsey Quarterly*, 2: 27–45.

McGregor, Doug (1960) *The Human Side of Enterprise*. New York: McGraw-Hill.

Mehrabian, Albert and Epstein, Norman (1972) 'A measure of emotional empathy', *Journal of Personality*, 40: 525–43.

Mehrabian, Albert and Wiener, Morton (1967) 'Decoding of inconsistent communications', *Journal of Personality and Social Psychology*, 6(1): 109–14.

Mellers, Barbara, Hertwig, Ralph and Kahneman, Daniel (2001) 'Do frequency representations eliminate conjunction effects? An exercise in adversarial collaboration', *Psychological Science*, 12(4): 269–75.

Micale, Frances (2004) *Meetings Made Easy: The Ultimate Fix-It Guide*. Irvine, CA: Entrepreneur Press.

Moniz, Richard J. (2009) 'The use of case studies in library administration courses and work: student and practitioner insights', *Library Leadership & Management*, 23(2): 108–12.

Nelson, Bob (2005) *1001 Ways to Reward Employees*. New York: Workman Publishers.

Nicholson, N. (2003) 'How to motivate your problem people', *Harvard Business Review*, 81(1): 57–65.

OfficePro (2007) 'In-person communication is most effective', *OfficePro*, 67(8): 8.

Olorunsola, R. (2007) 'Motivating library staff: a look at Frederick Herzberg's motivating-hygiene theory', *Library Review*, 41(2): 25–8.

O'Reilly, Charles A. III, Chatman, Jennifer and Caldwell, David A. (1991) 'People and organizational culture: a profile comparison approach to assessing person-organization fit', *Academy of Management Journal*, 34(3): 487–516.

Oud, Joanne (2008) 'Adjusting to the workplace: transitions faced by new academic libraries', *College & Research Libraries*, 69(3): 252–66.

Parasuraman, A., Zeithaml, V.A. and Berry, L.L. (1985) 'A conceptual model of service quality and its implications for future research', *Journal of Marketing*, 49(4): 41–50.

Radford, Marie L. (1998) 'Approach or avoidance? The role of nonverbal communication in the academic library user's decision to initiate a reference encounter', *Library Trends*, 46(4): 699–717.

Recardo, Ronald and Jolly, Jennifer (1997) 'Organizational culture and teams', *SAM Advanced Management Journal*, 62: 4–7.

Robertson, J. (2006) 'Age is so often a state of mind', *Employee Benefits*, August: 4–5.

Schein, Edgar H. (2004) *Organizational Culture and Leadership*. San Francisco, CA: Jossey-Bass.

Selberg, Roxanne (2009) 'Organizational culture challenge: don't let our differences keep us apart', *Technicalities*, 29(1): 11–14.

Shaughnessy, Thomas W. (1988) 'Organizational culture in libraries: some management perspectives', *Journal of Library Administration*, 9(3): 5–10.

Shepard, Jon M. and Hougland, James G. Jr (1978) 'Contingency theory: "complex man" or "complex organization"?', *Academy of Management Review*, 4(4): 413–27.

Snyder, Carolyn A. (2002) 'Measuring library service quality with a focus on the LibQUAL+ project: an interview with Fred Heath', *Library Administration & Management*, 16: 4–7.

Strategic Direction (2009) 'Social networking and the workplace: making the most of Web 2.0 technologies', *Strategic Direction*, 25(8): 20–3.

Sutton, Robert (2007) *The No Asshole Rule: Building a Civilized Workplace and Surviving One that Isn't*. New York: Warner Business Books.

Taylor, Frederick W. ([1911] 1947) *The Principles of Scientific Management*. New York: W.W. Norton.

Thaler, Richard H. and Sunstein, Cass R. (2008) *Nudge: Improving Decisions about Health, Wealth, and Happiness*. New York: Penguin Books.

Thomas, David J. and Ely, Robin A. (2001) *Harvard Business Review on Diversity*. Boston, MA: Harvard Business Review Press.

Thompson, Bruce, Cook, Carol and Heath, Fred (2001) 'How many dimensions does it take to measure users' perceptions of libraries? A LibQUAL+ study', *Libraries and the Academy*, 1(2): 129–38.

Van Maanen, John (1978) 'People processing: strategies of organizational socialization', *Organizational Dynamics*, 7(1): 18–36.

Verespej, Michael (1997) 'Zero tolerance', *Industry Week*, 246(1): 24–7.

Vroom, Victor ([1964] 1995) *Work and Motivation*. New York: Jossey-Bass.

Vroom, Victor and Jago, Arthur G. (1988) 'Managing participation: a critical dimension of leadership', *Journal of Management Development*, 7(5): 32–42.

Vroom, Victor and Jago, Arthur G. (2007) 'The role of situation in leadership', *American Psychologist*, 62(1): 17–24.

Weber, Max ([1922] 1978) *Economy and Society*, translated by Guenther Roth and Claus Wittich. Berkeley, CA: University of California Press.

Wellner, Alison S. (2005) 'Lost in translation', *Inc.*, 27(9): 37–8.

Wolf, William B. (1973) 'The impact of Kurt Lewin on management thought', *Academy of Management Proceedings*, August: 322–5.

Index